The Blackthorn Villagers' Cookery Book

A collection of recipes from the residents and friends of Blackthorn Village in Oxfordshire.

Edited by Sandie Stevenson

Published by Willow Pond
First Edition 2009

Foreword

Dear Fellow Cook,

What you hold in your hand is not simply a book of recipes; it is a collection of memories. Food so often has the ability to stir the soul and each recipe in this book is a little piece of history. Take for example the 'Gammon in Claret' and imagine tucking in to this medieval dish. Handed down from generation to generation this collection represents the family favourites of over 100 residents and friends of Blackthorn Village.

Located in rural North East Oxfordshire, Blackthorn is quiet and picturesque; swans, geese and ducks have made their home at the village pond, daffodils welcome Spring visitors through the white gates and the sounds of children playing can be heard in the streets.

Grounded in Celtic history settled by the Romans and overrun by the Saxons, Blackthorn was then lost to history until the late 16th century, when the notable game of 'running at the quintain' was played on its common land. A hamlet of neighbouring parish Ambrosden, Blackthorn did not become a village in its own right until Queen Elizabeth I sold it to John Denton of Ambrosden for a 'princely' sum of £612 3s. 9d.

Throughout the 17th, 18th and 19th centuries Blackthorn had prosperous local businesses a chapel and school and was a thriving farming community. Many of the recipes within this book reflect this heritage, like the 'Almond Shortbread', the secret family recipe which we now share with you.

As a resident, I can tell you first hand that nowadays Blackthorn is a very different village. Gone are the butcher, the baker, the candlestick maker. All that remains are the houses that bear the names of these former businesses. The Old Bake House, dating back to the 16th century, adorns the cover of this book.

One thing that has not changed is the sense of community spirit, which is still at the heart of the village. This more than anything has inspired us to come together to produce this cookery book. From the old traditional favourites to bang up to date modern microwave cookery all are included; yes you really are only 5 minutes away from a chocolate cake any time of the day or night!

Our aim is simple; we would like to create a 21st century play area for the children of Blackthorn to enjoy and all proceeds from the sale will go towards this goal. From toddlers to teenagers none have been forgotten. Our plans are made our targets are set, and the team is itching to break ground on the project.

Thank you for supporting our cause by buying this book. We hope you have fun trying out our recipes and creating memories of your own. Indulge!

Sandie Stevenson
On behalf of the Blackthorn Recreational Park Committee

Contents

"My doctor told me to stop having intimate dinners for four.

Unless...
　　　　there are three other people"

Orson Welles, (1915 - 1985)

Starters
- Soups

Spicy Beetroot and Chilli

Submitted by Anne and Andy Lee, Blackthorn

1 lb raw beetroot (peeled
and chopped)
1 large onion (diced)
1 small red chilli
2 cloves of garlic

2 tsp of curry powder
Tin of tomatoes
Olive oil/butter
Water/vegetable stock

Cook on hob
Large saucepan
Blender

Serves 4-6

Method

Fry the onion, garlic and chilli until soft. Add the curry powder
and fry for a further minute. Add the beetroot and the tomatoes.
Cover with water/vegetable stock. Cook gently until beetroot is
tender. Blend in a liquidiser and add more water if necessary.

Recipe Background

A glut of home grown beetroot meant finding new ways to cook
it. Having found a recipe for beetroot soup we have adapted
and changed it to suit our taste. It is very hot and spicy so if you
want a milder version reduce the chilli and curry powder.

Celeriac, Bramley Apple and Stilton

Submitted by Keith and Caroline Crampton, Blackthorn

1 oz butter
2 tbsp olive oil
1 lb celeriac (peeled and cubed)
1 large onion (chopped)

¼ pt dry cider
3½ oz apples (diced)
1¾ pt chicken stock
5 fl oz single cream
4 oz Stilton cheese (crumbled)
Salt and pepper (to taste)

Cook on hob
Blender
Heavy bottomed non-stick saucepan

Method

In a pan, heat the butter with the oil and fry the celeriac until lightly golden. Add the onion and cook for 3-4 minutes.
Pour in the cider and stock and bring to the boil. Reduce heat and cook until celeriac is tender (20-25 minutes). Add the apples and cook for a further 3-4 minutes. Remove from heat and pour into a blender and blend until smooth. Immediately before serving, melt the Stilton in the cream and stir into the warm soup.

Soupe aux Moules

Submitted by Virginie Halphen, Blackthorn

1 kg mussels
1 bunch of sorrel
40 g butter
2 egg yolks
20 cl single cream
3 tbsp flour

1 bay leaf
1 tsp thyme
20 cl white wine (Muscadet is fine)
Salt and pepper

Cook on hob
Large saucepan

Serves 4-6

Method

Scrub and wash the mussels and put them in a large saucepan with the white wine, the thyme and the bay leaf. Cook them over a brisk heat until they are all opened. Take them out of their shells. Filter the cooking juice through a strainer lined with muslin. Wash the sorrel and mince it. Melt 20 g of butter in a saucepan and fry the sorrel in it for 3-4 minutes. Melt the remaining butter and add the flour, stir into the cooking juice of the mussels and add some water to get 1 litre of liquid. Bring to the boil gently. Mix the egg yolk with the cream in a saucepan, add the mussels and the sorrel and heat gently without boiling. Taste and adjust the seasoning. Serve very hot.

Ruth's Lentil

Submitted by Ruth Harris, CAFE, Friend of Blackthorn

2 oz margarine
8 oz red lentils
1 medium onion (peeled and sliced)
3 carrots (peeled and sliced)
2 medium potatoes (peeled and sliced)
6 oz swede/turnip (peeled and sliced)

2½ pt stock (stock cubes)
½ pt milk
Chopped parsley
Chilli powder
(to taste - optional)
Snippets of cooked bacon (an optional extra)

Serves 6

Cook on hob
Food processor
Heavy bottomed non-stick saucepan

Method

Melt the margarine in a large saucepan. Add the lentils, onion, carrots, potatoes and swede/turnip. Stir them over a low heat. Add the stock and bring to the boil. Simmer until tender. Cool. Liquidise in a food processor. Return to the pan and add the milk, season to taste. Add chilli powder, about half a teaspoonful or more!!! Add bacon and garnish with parsley.

Chunky Italian Vegetable

Submitted by Doreen Shirley, Friend of Blackthorn

2 carrots
1 onion
2 celery sticks
200 g turnip/swede
1 garlic clove (crushed)
2 x 400 g cans of chopped tomatoes

1 tbsp tomato puree
1 tbsp Italian dried mixed herbs
900 ml hot vegetable stock

Cook on hob
Large saucepan

Method

Chop the carrots, onion, celery sticks and turnip/swede into small pieces. Put them into a large saucepan with the crushed garlic clove, chopped tomatoes, tomato puree and herbs. Pour in the stock, and then simmer until all the vegetables are tender (about 25-30 minutes). Season, then serve topped with a few basil leaves, if you have some.

This is like Minestrone, without the pasta!

Carrot and Orange

Submitted by Nina Chadbone, Blackthorn

25 g butter
600 g carrots (sliced)
1 medium potato (peeled and sliced)
1 shallot (chopped)

2 tsp sugar
1 ltr chicken/vegetable stock
Grated zest and juice from 2 oranges
150 ml double cream

Cook on hob
Large saucepan
Blender

Serves 4

Method

Melt the butter in a pan and then add the carrots, potato and shallot. Stir well to make sure they are all coated in the butter. Cover and cook over a low heat for about 10 minutes, stirring occasionally. Add the sugar and stock and turn the heat up until simmering. Simmer for 15 minutes. Add the orange juice and zest. Puree the soup and then add two thirds of the cream. Reheat the soup but do not allow to boil. When ready to serve pour into bowls and using the remaining cream add a swirl of cream in the middle, sprinkle with black pepper and serve with warm crusty bread.

Pea and Spinach

Submitted by Bruce Knox, Blackthorn

1 lb peas (fresh)
1 bunch spring onions
1 round lettuce (chopped)
2 generous handfuls of fresh
spinach leaves
1 pt vegetable stock

1 oz butter
1 level tsp caster sugar
1 clove garlic
Salt and pepper (to taste)
1 small tub fromage frais

Cook on hob
Frying pan
Saucepan
Blender

Serves 4

Method

Peel the garlic and chop. Slice the spring onions. Soften them in a frying pan by heating in butter for 3 minutes, seasoning with pepper. Add the peas and turn for 30 seconds. Add stock, spinach leaves, lettuce, sugar, salt and pepper and bring to the boil. Simmer for roughly 5 minutes. Cool slightly and then put through a blender or transfer to a warm pan and blend with a hand blender. Garnish with either fromage frais, parsley or mint leaves.

Recipe Background

Home-made pea soup was a favourite snack served by my grandmother to visitors on Hogmanay and first footers after 12 midnight. I added spinach one day as we had some left-overs and really liked the taste it brings to the peas.

Honey Roasted Swede

Submitted by Doreen Shirley, Friend of Blackthorn

500 g swede (peeled and cubed)
1 onion (peeled and chopped)
120 g carrots (peeled and chopped)

75 g celery (chopped)
1 tbsp clear honey
75 g crème fraiche

Preheat oven to 200C
Cook on hob
Roasting tin
Saucepan
Blender

Serves 4

Method

Place the swede in a roasting tin. Mist with low fat cooking spray and bake for 30 minutes. Mist a pan with low fat spray and add the onion, carrots and celery. Fry for 15 minutes and set aside. Drizzle the honey over the swede and cook for a further 10 minutes. Add the swede to the vegetables with the hot vegetable stock, fresh thyme leaves and crème fraiche. Simmer for 10 minutes, and then blend until smooth. Season with nutmeg and warm through. Ladle into 4 bowls and top each with 1 tsp crème fraiche and thyme leaves.

Roasted Red Pepper

Submitted by Karen Jobling, Blackthorn

4 red peppers (deseeded)
1 medium carrot
1 small parsnip
2 medium onions
1 tbsp balsamic vinegar

2 tbsp olive oil
1 ltr vegetable stock
Dash of Tabasco sauce
Salt and pepper

Preheat oven to 190C
Roasting tray
Blender

Serves 4

Method

Roughly chop the peppers, carrot, parsnip and onions and place on a roasting tray. Drizzle the olive oil and balsamic vinegar all over, add the dash of Tabasco. Season with salt and pepper to taste. Roast the vegetables until tender for approximately 30 minutes. Turn the vegetables half way through cooking.
Put roasted vegetables and their juices, into a blender and blitz until smooth. Add the hot stock to the soup. Serve with a dollop of soured cream and crusty bread.

Julienne

Submitted by Doreen Shirley, Friend of Blackthorn

1½ pt stock/water
1 small parsnip
1 tsp yeast extract
1 small leek

1 oz butter/fat
2-3 celery stalks
1 small carrot
salt (to taste)

Cook on hob
Saucepan

Serves 6

Method

Clean the vegetables. Peel the carrot and parsnip.
Scrub the celery and leeks. Cut the vegetables in julienne strips
(^{1}/$_2$ inch by 1 inch long). Mix the stock with yeast extract, butter
and salt and bring to the boil. Add the vegetable strips and boil
for about 20 minutes. All vegetables should be soft but not
broken up.

Soupe á L'oignon Gratinée

Submitted by Virginie Halphen, Blackthorn

25 g butter
300 g onions
25 g flour
2 ltr water
1 chicken stock cube
50 ml red wine

Salt and pepper
1 bay leaf
4 slices stale bread/bread
dried in oven
50 g Emmental cheese
(grated)

Cook on hob
Finish under grill
Large saucepan

Serves 4

Method

Peel and cut the onions into thin strips. Slice the bread. Melt
the butter in a large saucepan. Fry the onions in the butter
until golden (don't let them go dark!). Add the flour, stir to
incorporate the flour and add the water slowly, then the stock
cube, the red wine, salt and pepper and the bay leaf. Leave to
simmer for about 15 minutes. Discard the bay leaf . Pour the
soup into 4 earthenware dishes. Toast the slices of bread and
put them on top of the soup. Cover the bread with the grated
Emmental and cook under the grill. Serve immediately.

Recipe Background

The 'soupe á l'oignon gratinée' is from Paris and owes its reputation to the 'bistrots' (pubs) of Les Halles, old Parisian covered market and Montmatre the artists' district. By tradition this soup is eaten by the night birds very early in the morning to avoid hangover!

Pea and Garlic

Submitted by Sue and Andy Sparkes, Blackthorn

2 heads of garlic
4 tsp olive oil
400 g frozen peas
50 g butter
4 tbsp Parmesan (grated)
400 ml vegetable/chicken
stock (or stock from ham
hocks)

300 ml double cream
Truffle oil to drizzle over
before serving (optional)
A small handful or two of
cooked diced ham hock
(optional)

Preheat oven to 200C
Saucepan
Food processor or blender

Serves 4

Method

Slice the top of the heads of garlic: you want to see the tops of the cloves just revealed in cross section. Cut out a square of foil large enough to make a baggy parcel around the garlic. Sit the garlic in the middle of the foil and drizzle with olive oil. Make a loose parcel around the garlic sealing the edges of the foil. Put in the oven for 1 hour (until soft). Cook the peas in boiling salted water. Drain and tip into a food processor. Squeeze in the soft cooked cloves of garlic. Add the butter and Parmesan and about a ½ of the stock (depending on the size of the processor or blender) Process to a creamy puree. Pour the mixture into a saucepan and add the remaining stock and ham. Bring up to a slow simmer. Check the flavour and add cream to taste. Heat gently, season to taste with salt and pepper and serve. Drizzle with truffle oil if required.

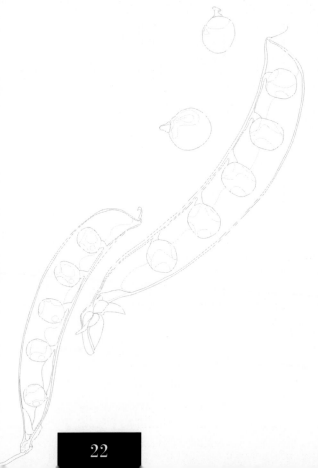

Leek and Potato

Submitted by Doreen Shirley, Friend of Blackthorn

2 leeks
½ pt full fat milk/single cream
1 medium potato
1½ pt water

1 oz margarine
1-2 tbsp chopped parsley
1 bay leaf
Salt and pepper

Cook on hob
Saucepan
Blender or sieve

Serves 4

Method

Wash and chop the leeks, discarding the tough green leaves, but using as much of the green part as possible. Peel and chop the potato. Cook these very gently in margarine together with the bay leaf, for about 10 minutes, stirring occasionally, but on no account let them brown. Add the water and cook gently for about 30 minutes, then sieve or liquidise. Return to the pan, and add the milk/cream, parsley and seasoning, but do not let it boil.

Serve with nice crusty bread!

Starters
- Breads

Quick Wholemeal

Submitted by Maureen Byrd, in memory of Michael Byrd, Blackthorn

1½ lb wholemeal flour
1 dsp salt
1 tbsp dried yeast (or 1 oz fresh)
1 tsp white/ brown sugar

¾ pt milk
¼ pt tepid water (this may vary depending on the brand of flour used)

Preheat oven to 205C
Loaf tins/baking trays

1 large and 1 small loaf

Method

Grease loaf tins/baking trays. Place the flour and salt in a bowl and stand in a warm place. Warm the milk to room temperature and put half into another bowl. Mix in the dried yeast and the sugar and leave in a warm place until the yeast has dissolved and begun to froth (if using fresh yeast it does not need to froth). Make a well in the centre of the flour and pour in the dissolved yeast mixture. Mix into a soft dough and gradually add the remaining milk and enough water to make an elastic dough. Turn dough out onto a floured board and knead lightly for 5 minutes. Divide the dough as required, mould slightly but do not over handle. Put into loaf tins/baking trays and cover with a clean tea towel or cling film.

Stand in a warm place and leave to rise (between 1-2 hours). Then bake in the centre of a preheated oven; cooking times vary depending on the size of the loaf (large 45 minutes, small 30 minutes and rolls 15 minutes). Test the loaves to see if they are cooked by tapping the bottom of them; a completely baked loaf will sound hollow. Once cooked turn out from tins and leave to cool.

Bread will keep for around 5 days.

Top Tip

When kneading the dough make sure you have warm hands. If the dough is left too long to rise it will drop back. Do not attempt to bake. Re-knead the dough and leave to rise again.

Zucchini Bread

Submitted by Susan McKinney, Blackthorn

2 cups sugar
3 cups flour
1¼ tsp salt
1 tsp bicarbonate of soda
1 tsp cinnamon
¼ tsp baking powder
¾ pt milk
3 tsp vanilla extract

¼ pt tepid water (this may
vary depending on the brand
of flour used)
2 cups chopped zucchini
(courgettes)
3 eggs
1 cup vegetable oil

Preheat oven to 160C
Blender
2 loaf tins

Method

Separately put the wet ingredients into a blender and liquidise.
Combine the dry ingredients with the wet ingredients. Divide
into 2 greased loaf tins. Bake for 1 hour. Remove from pans
immediately to cool.

.

Starters
- Appetisers

Tuna with Red Onion and Salad

Submitted by Daphne Donnelly, Blackthorn

2 large tins of tuna (your choice but in oil is best)
2 red onions
1 tin borlotti beans
1 tin cannellini beans

1 large packet of mixed leaf salad
Olive oil and balsamic vinegar dressing
Salt and black pepper

Method

Cover a flat large serving plate with Italian mixed salad leaves. Drain and rinse the borlotti and cannellini beans. Mix the beans and put as a layer on top of the salad leaves (leaving a border of leaves around the outside). Drain the tuna and place on top of the beans. Chop red onions into fine rings and place on top of the tuna, each time the layer on top is slightly smaller than the one below. Finally, add salt and pepper and cover with the olive oil and balsamic vinegar dressing just before serving. Serve with some crusty bread or some really nice different types of Italian bread. Terrific for the centre of the table for several people to share.

.

Crab Spring Rolls

Submitted by Sue and Andy Sparkes, Blackthorn

8 large spring roll wrappers
(about 25 cm square)
1 large egg white
(for brushing)
Groundnut oil
(for deep frying)
250 g white crab meat
2 spring onions (trimmed and
finely sliced)

Small handful of coriander
leaves (chopped)
1 tbsp wholegrain mustard
1 ½ tbsp mayonnaise
Smoked sea salt and black
pepper
Squeeze of lime juice

Cook on hob
Pan suitable for deep frying

Serves 4

Method

For the filling, toss all the ingredients together in a bowl until
evenly combined. Add salt, pepper and lime juice to taste.
Lay a spring roll wrapper on a board with a corner facing you
(keep the rest covered with a tea towel to prevent them drying
out). Spoon 2 tbsp of the crab meat filling on to the bottom
of the wrapper, and then brush the surrounding pastry with
egg white. Fold the bottom edge up over the filling, brush the
sides with more egg white and fold them in over the filling,

like an envelope. Roll up into a log. Repeat with the rest of the wrappers and filling.

Heat the oil for deep frying in a suitable pan. To check the oil is hot enough, drop in a cube of bread; it should sizzle vigorously. Deep fry the rolls in batches for 40-60 seconds until golden brown and crisp. Drain on kitchen paper. Cut the spring rolls in half on the diagonal and serve warm, with a bowl of sweet chilli sauce for dipping.

Salmon Mousse

Submitted by Hilary Coldicott, Friend of Blackthorn

2 tbsp water (boiled)
2 tsp gelatine
1 tin salmon (drained)
2 tbsp lemon juice
1 tsp tomato puree

1 tbsp chopped parsley
¼ pt double cream
1 egg white
Salt and pepper

Whisk
Oiled mould

Method

Dissolve the gelatine in the water and leave to cool. Remove the skin and bones from fish and mash into a smooth paste. Stir in the lemon juice and parsley and season with salt and pepper. Mix in the cooled gelatine. Whisk the cream and fold into the salmon mix. Whisk the egg white until stiff and fold in. Turn out into mould and chill.

Baked Crab Cakes

Submitted by Helen Prince, Friend of Blackthorn

1 cup mayonnaise
¼ cup spicy brown mustard
2 tbsp Worcestershire sauce
1 egg (beaten)
1-2 tsp hot red pepper sauce
(optional)

2 lb lump crab meat
3-3½ cups fresh breadcrumbs
¼ tsp salt or to taste
1 tsp Old Bay seasoning
Cracker crumbs

Preheat oven to 200C
Mixing bowl
Rimmed baking sheet

Method

In a bowl mix the mayo, mustard, Worcestershire sauce, hot
sauce, and egg until just combined. Set aside (may cover and
refrigerate for no more than 24 hrs). Place the crab meat in
a strainer to remove excess water, allowing it to drain for 10
minutes then transfer to a large bowl, being careful not to break
up the big pieces. Add half a cup of breadcrumbs to the crab
meat and mix gently. Spray a rimmed baking sheet with nonstick
spray or line with parchment paper. Using a spatula, fold in
about 1 cup of the mayo mixture. Season to taste. Add 2 to 3

cups of breadcrumbs to the crab meat, being careful not to over mix. Test a small portion to see if it holds together. If not, add the remaining half cup of the mayo mixture, 1 to 2 tbsp at a time. If the mixture is too wet, add the remaining quarter cup of breadcrumbs in the same manner. Form each crab cake to the desired size (a 6 oz dinner portion will fill the palm of your hand). Lightly cover the crab cake with cracker crumbs or dry breadcrumbs. Bake for 10-12 minutes until golden brown. For an extra crisp top, grill for 1 minute.

Calamari Tapas

Submitted by Sue and Andy Sparkes, Blackthorn

Extra virgin olive oil
1 bunch of fresh rosemary
2 red chillies (deseeded and
finely chopped)
150 ml single cream
3 egg yolks
2 tbsp Parmesan (grated)
2 tbsp plain flour

Salt and ground black pepper
1 garlic clove (peeled and
crushed)
1 tsp dried oregano
Vegetable oil (for deep-frying)
6 squid (cleaned and cut into
rings)

Cook on hob
Pan for deep-frying to 200C
Small saucepan

Method

For the dressing: warm the olive oil in a small pan and add the
rosemary and chilli and set aside. Pour the cream into a large
bowl and add the egg yolks, Parmesan, flour, garlic and oregano.
Beat until it becomes a smooth batter and season. Heat the oil
for deep-frying to 200C, or until a cube of bread browns in 30
seconds. Dip the squid rings into the batter, one at a time, and
place gently into the oil. Fry for 2-3 minutes until golden brown.
Drain on kitchen paper and serve immediately, drizzled with the
dressing. Add salt if required.

Fresh Mussels (Moules) with Cider and White Wine

Submitted by Sue and Andy Sparkes, Blackthorn

2 kg mussels
20 g butter
1 garlic clove (finely chopped)
4 shallots/1 small onion (finely chopped)

½ bulb of fennel (finely chopped)
100 ml dry white wine
100 ml Blackthorn cider
A handful of parsley leaves
Salt and pepper (to taste)

Cook on hob
Large saucepan

Serves 4

Method

Wash the mussels under plenty of cold running water. Discard any broken or open ones that do not close when lightly squeezed or tapped. Pull out the tough fibrous beards protruding from between the tightly closed shells. Knock off or scrape off with a knife any barnacles and then give the mussels another quick rinse to remove any little pieces of shell. Soften the garlic, shallots and fennel in the butter, until lightly golden, in a large pan big enough to take all the mussels - it should only be half full. Add the cider and wine and bring up to a light simmer. Add the mussels and bring the heat up slightly, then cover and steam them in their own juices for 3-4 minutes. Give the pan a good shake every now and then. Once the mussels have opened remove with a slotted spoon and put to one side in a warmed covered dish, leaving all the liquid in the pot. Bring to the boil then reduce to a simmer, whisk in a large knob of butter. Taste and season to your own palate. Return the mussels to the pan and add the parsley and stir through to make sure all the mussels get a good coating of the juices. Remove from the heat and spoon into warmed bowls and serve with lots of warm crusty bread. Discard any mussels that have not opened during cooking.

Smoked Salmon Pate

Submitted by The Lamonts, Blackthorn

4 oz butter
8 oz smoked salmon (plus extra to garnish)
1 tbsp lemon juice
Salt and pepper (to season)

½ pt double cream (lightly whipped)/small tub of crème fraiche
Thinly sliced cucumber (to garnish

Blender

Method

Melt the butter and allow to cool for 5 minutes. Place the smoked salmon in a blender with the melted butter and mix to a smooth paste. Season with salt and pepper and lemon juice, then mix in the cream. Spoon the pate into a serving dish and garnish with the extra smoked salmon and cucumber. Chill for 30 minutes before serving. This makes an excellent starter served with crusty bread or multigrain crackers!

Top Tip

Use crème fraiche instead of cream if you are counting the calories. If you're looking to impress: thinly slice a cucumber lengthways and line a terrine with the slices, before you spoon in the pate; this looks stunning when turned out onto a plate.

Summer Ceviche

Submitted by Nick Crutch, Friend of Blackthorn

8 oz prawns
8 oz scallops (cut into ¼ inch pieces)
8 oz sea bass (cut into ¼ inch pieces)
½ cup fresh lime juice
¼ cup fresh orange juice
¼ cup fresh lemon juice
1 tbsp fresh garlic (minced)

1 cup cherry tomatoes (quartered)
¼ cup red onion (diced)
1 medium jalapeno pepper (minced)
1 tbsp extra virgin olive oil
1 medium avocado (sliced)
¼ cup fresh coriander (chopped)
1 lettuce

Medium sized stock pot
Large shallow bowl

Serves 4

Method

Add the prawns and scallops to a pot of boiling salted water and cook for 1 minute. Plunge prawns and scallops into a bowl of very cold water to stop the cooking process. Drain well. Cut the prawns lengthways in half. Combine the prawns, scallops and sea bass in a large shallow bowl. Season with a little salt and pepper. Combine the juices and garlic and pour over the seafood mixture. Toss to coat. Cover and refrigerate for 2 hours, stirring occasionally. Add the tomatoes, onion, jalapeno and olive oil and gently mix. Marinate for at least another hour until the fish is opaque. Stir in the coriander. Serve with avocado slices on a bed of lettuce, spooning a little of the marinade over each portion.

After a tough summer workout, I ensure that I replace carbohydrate with energy drinks. Then within the hour I sit down to this meal, which is just bursting with flavours!

Smoked Salmon Soufflés

Submitted by Susan Henderson, Blackthorn

40 g butter
40 g plain flour
350 ml milk
3 large eggs (separated)
55 g Gruyere cheese (finely grated)
150 g smoked salmon (chopped)

3 tbsp crème fraiche
1 tsp vodka
1 tbsp chopped dill
2 tbsp olive oil
1 tbsp lemon juice
Sprigs of dill to garnish
Assorted green salad leaves to serve

Preheat oven to 200C
Saucepan
6 Ramekin dishes (buttered and lined with grease proof paper)
Whisk
Roasting tin

Serves 4

Method

Melt the butter in a pan, remove from heat and add flour. Stir to make a thick paste and gradually add milk. Return to the heat and continue to add the milk, stirring continuously until it is smooth and thickened, mixture should not boil. Remove from the heat and beat in the egg yolks, cheese and chopped dill. Stir in the smoked salmon (leave some for garnishing) and season.

Whisk the egg whites until stiff and fold into the salmon mix with a metal spoon. Spoon the mixture into the ramekins and place in a roasting tin half filled with water. Bake for 15-20 minutes until well risen and golden. Remove from oven and leave to cool, soufflés will sink a little when they cool, this is normal. Once cooled remove from the ramekins and place onto a sheet of grease proof paper, cover and chill. Mix the crème fraiche and vodka together. Whisk the olive oil and lemon juice together to make a quick salad dressing. To serve: top each soufflé with a little of the vodka crème fraiche and a sprig of dill and bake at 200C for approx 10 minutes. Arrange the salad leaves on a plate, drizzle over the dressing and place the soufflés on top, scatter the remaining salmon over the top to garnish; serve warm.

Top Tip

Soufflés can be made up to 2 days before.

Ham Stuffed Peaches

Submitted by Susan Henderson, Blackthorn

1 16 oz tin of peaches
4 oz sliced cooked ham
4 tbsp mayonnaise
2 tsp chopped parsley

Salt and pepper
Few lettuce leaves and more
parsley

Method

Strain the juice from the peaches and drain on kitchen roll.
Mince ham finely and mix with mayonnaise and parsley, season
to taste. Pipe or spoon the ham mixture into peach cavity.
Arrange on bed of lettuce and garnish with extra parsley.

Potatoes with Sausages Tapas

Submitted by Sue and Andy Sparkes, Blackthorn

12 small/new potatoes (about
50 g each)
12 small sausages
4 tbsp olive oil
1 tsp smoked paprika

1 tbsp chopped fresh parsley
2 cloves garlic
(finely chopped)
Sea salt

Preheat the oven to 200C
Roasting tin

Method

Using an apple corer or a sharp small knife, make a hole
through the centre of each potato. Place a sausage in each
one. Reserve the cut-out pieces of potato. Put the oil into a
roasting tin, lightly season with salt, sprinkle in half the parsley,
half the garlic and the smoked paprika. Add the potatoes with
sausages and the reserved potato pieces. Mix together gently
with your hands, making sure the potatoes get a coating of all
the ingredients. Roast for 15 minutes, then turn the potatoes
over and add the remaining parsley and garlic and baste with the
oil. Return the tin to the oven and continue roasting (for about
30 minutes). Turn and baste three or four more times. Serve
immediately in a warm serving dish.

Salt and Chilli Chicken Wings

Submitted by Joe Kong, Blackthorn

12 chicken wings
Cornflour
½ tsp salt
1 pinch five spice
4 gloves garlic (finely chopped)

2 Thai chillies (finely chopped)
1 spring onion (finely chopped)
Oil

Preheat oven 220C
Oven rack
Oven drip tray
Wok

Method

Lightly coat chicken wings in cornflour and place on a rack high over a drip tray into the oven for 10 minutes (add an extra 5 minutes if they are from big chickens). Rotate the wings (move the wings in the front to the back of the oven) and cook for a further 5 minutes. Remove chicken from oven and heat a couple of drops of oil in a wok at 120C. Add garlic and chilli and stir for 10 seconds. Turn heat off and add chicken wings and the spring onion, swish and throw the contents about without spillage. Sprinkle the salt and five spice, swish and throw, serve.

Recipe Background

This is a popular Cantonese starter in which the chicken is normally deep fried. However, I find this too greasy and messy in a domestic kitchen. I analysed the cooking process and came up with this technique which avoids the need to deep fat fry. This recipe I dedicate to all the mums out there.

Blue Cheese Baked Mushrooms

Submitted by Ruth and Tim Harvey, Blackthorn

Nice big field mushrooms
(one per person)
Any blue cheese
Parma ham

Preheat oven to 150C

Method

Upturn mushrooms, take out stalks, fill with cheese and wrap
with ham. Pop in oven for 10-15 minutes. Serve with a green
salad. Couldn't be easier but tastes divine!

Chorizo Sausage Tapas

Submitted by Sue and Andy Sparkes, Blackthorn

250 g cherry tomatoes
4 tbsp balsamic vinegar
2 tbsp olive oil

1 tsp chopped thyme
Salt and ground black pepper
4 slices of chorizo sausage

Preheat oven to 200C
Roasting dish
Heavy-based non-stick frying pan

Serves 4

Method

Place the cherry tomatoes in a roasting tray. Toss with 2 tbsp of balsamic vinegar, olive oil and thyme and season with salt and freshly ground pepper. Roast for 5-10 minutes, until softened. Heat frying pan over medium heat until hot. Add the chorizo to the pan and sear for 1 minute on each side. Divide the roast tomatoes and seared chorizo among four serving plates. Drizzle the remaining balsamic vinegar around each portion and serve.

Sandie's Low Calorie Cream Cheese

Submitted by Sandie Stevenson, Blackthorn

1 small pot of Greek yoghurt
1 small pot of quark (curd cheese)
2 spring onions/1 tbsp of chives (finely chopped)
2 tsp parsley (finely chopped)

1 tsp tarragon
1 tsp thyme
2 cloves of garlic (peeled and finely chopped)
Pepper and salt

Pretty serving bowl
Blender

Method

Blend all the ingredients together until smooth and lump free. Serve with seeded bread or a French stick and a glass of red wine.

Top Tip

This recipe is a low calorie alternative to full fat cream cheese and is suitable for vegetarians too. If you can't find curd cheese then use cottage cheese instead. This makes a great dinner party starter and can be whipped up in a matter of minutes; alternatively serve with crackers just before coffee and mints.

Melon Boats

Submitted by Brandon Lamont, Blackthorn

1 honeydew melon
2 large oranges

Cocktail sticks   Serves 4-8

Method

Cut the melon in half and scoop out the seeds, then cut in half
again or into quarters, depending on how many people you are
serving. Prepare the melon by slicing all the way through each
piece as if removing the rind then cut into segments. Cut the
oranges into even slices, cut some of these in half. Put the semi
circles of orange between each melon segment. Skewer the
whole orange slices and stick into the melon to make sails.

Top Tip

This makes a great starter or pud and is fun and easy to make;
it also looks good on the plate! Remember to get a grown up to
help with the cutting! For a bit of an added twist you can serve
with Italian hams and other fruits or ice cream if you're having it
as a pudding.

Recipe Background

Last Christmas my Grandma made this as a starter, because I didn't like what the grown ups were having. Now every time I have melon boats I think of Christmas and presents; especially presents.

Tomato Tart

Submitted by Jenny Boyd, Friend of Blackthorn

500 g ready to roll puff pastry | Salt and pepper
300 g cherry tomatoes | Parmesan cheese
Olive tapenade | Fresh basil
Olive oil

Preheat oven to 200C   Serves 4
Baking tin

Roll the puff pastry to line a 12 x 35 cm tin. Spread the base generously with the olive tapenade. Cut the cherry tomatoes in half and closely pack the tin with the tomatoes, cut side down. Season with salt and pepper and drizzle with olive oil. Sprinkle over a generous helping of grated Parmesan and torn basil leaves. Bake for 20 minutes in a preheated oven. Serve warm with a green salad.

Hot Stuffed Avocado

Submitted by Christine Neville, Friend of Blackthorn

1 small onion (peeled and chopped)
1 tbsp oil
1 ripe avocado
1 tsp lemon juice
2 tomatoes (chopped)
2 tbsp natural yoghurt
2 tbsp mayonnaise

¼ level tsp ready made mustard
1 inch of cucumber (peeled and diced)
Salt and pepper
1 oz mozzarella cheese
1 oz walnuts
Chives and lemon (to garnish)

Cook in microwave

Serves 4

Method

Put the onion and oil in a basin and microwave on high for 3 minutes or until soft. Meanwhile, halve and stone the avocado. Using a teaspoon, scoop out most of the flesh into a bowl, leaving a third of an inch thick shell. Sprinkle the inside of the shell with lemon juice. Mash the scooped out flesh to a pulp. Stir in the tomatoes, yoghurt, mayonnaise, mustard, cucumber, salt and pepper and mix thoroughly. Put the avocado shells on to a serving plate and fill with tomato mixture. Arrange small pieces of cheese over the top, and sprinkle with walnuts. Microwave on high for 2–3 minutes or until warmed through. Garnish with chives and lemon segments.

Beetroot and Shallot Tarte Tatin

Submitted by Caroline Crampton, Blackthorn

1 lb raw beetroot (peeled and chopped into 2.5 cm chunks)
12 oz large shallots
8 oz puff pastry
2 oz unsalted butter (softened)

3 oz caster sugar
2 tbsp balsamic vinegar
Salt and pepper
Chopped flat leaf parsley (optional)

Preheat oven to 220C
Saucepan
10 inch oven proof non-stick frying pan

Serves 6

Method

Put the beetroot chunks into a pan of lightly salted water and bring to the boil. Simmer for 30-40 minutes until just tender. Place the whole shallots into a pan of boiling water and simmer for 10 minutes; drain and leave to cool then peel off skins and outer layers. Spread the butter over the inside of the frying pan and sprinkle over the sugar. Arrange pieces of beetroot and shallots on top and season with salt and pepper. Place the frying pan over a medium heat and cook for 15-20 minutes until the butter and sugar have caramelised. Roll out the pastry into a circle 2 inches wider than the frying pan (12 inches). Add the balsamic vinegar to the caramelised beetroot and shallots. Lay the pastry over the frying pan making sure the excess is tucked inside the pan. Prick the top of the pastry and cook for approx 35 minutes, until golden brown. Cool for 5 minutes and then place an inverted serving plate over the frying pan and turn out. The pastry should be on the bottom if done correctly. Sprinkle with parsley (optional) and serve with a fresh green salad.

Bon Appétit!

Tre-colore Starter

Submitted by The Lamonts, Blackthorn

Buffalo mozzarella
Tomatoes
Avocado
Olive oil
Balsamic vinegar

Method   Serves 4

Slice the mozzarella, tomatoes and avocado evenly. Layer on a
serving plate. Mix together the olive oil and vinegar and drizzle
over.

Top Tip

Serve with crusty bread. This recipe also makes a great salad! If
you don't like avocado use rocket instead.

Chick Pea and Spinach Tapas

Submitted by Sue and Andy Sparkes, Blackthorn

6 tbsp of olive oil
3 slices white bread
(crusts removed and cubed)
3 garlic cloves (thinly sliced)
1 tsp ground cumin
1 tbsp red wine

800 g canned chick peas
(rinsed and drained)
450 g fresh spinach
Smoked sea salt and black
pepper

Cook on hob
Large heavy based frying pan
Pestle and mortar or food processor

Serves 4

Method

Heat the olive oil in a large, heavy-based frying pan over a
medium heat. Add the bread and fry for 5 minutes until golden
brown on all sides. Add the garlic and cumin and cook for 1-2
minutes, until the garlic is nutty brown. Transfer to a pestle
and mortar or food processor. Add the vinegar and mash or
process to a paste. Return the bread paste to the pan and add
the drained chick peas. Cook, stirring, until the chick peas have
absorbed the flavours and are hot, then season with sea salt and
freshly ground pepper. If the consistency is a little thick, add
some water. Now add the spinach and cook until just wilted,
around 2 minutes. Check the seasoning and serve.

Melon and Goats' Cheese Salad

Submitted by Jenny Thompson, Blackthorn

Melon (ideally orange fleshed)
Cucumber (roughly 3 inches)
16 small tomatoes
100 g crumbly goats' cheese
1 tbsp fine shredded mint

3 tbsp olive oil
1 tbsp red wine vinegar
Pinch of caster sugar/½ tsp runny honey
1 tsp Dijon mustard
Pinch of salt and pepper

Method   Serves 2

Cut up melon so 6-8 slices on each plate fanned out, skin off.
Cut skin from cucumber and slice thinly and then in half;
sprinkle over melon. Cut tomatoes in half and spread over
melon. Crumble goats' cheese over the top, and then scatter
mint over too. For the dressing put the oil, red wine vinegar,
sugar, mustard, salt and pepper into a glass jar, twist on lid and
give a good shake to mix it all up. To serve, spoon over dressing.

Top Tip

A job of moments to put this great salad together with a delicious
melding of flavours to really get your taste buds going!
Why not try other dressings too, such as balsamic and olive

oil? We have this as a main course but can be served as a great starter too.

Recipe Background

This comes from our lovely friend Sarah who really doesn't 'do' cooking, but who once served this up as a starter and had us all smacking our lips wanting more!

Italian Bruschetta

Submitted by Rachel Lamont, Blackthorn

1 French stick
Olive oil
Fresh vine tomatoes (yellow, red and orange)
Handful of fresh basil (finely chopped)

1 red onion (finely chopped)
2 cloves of garlic (finely chopped)
Juice of 1 lemon
Salt and black pepper

Preheat oven to 180C

Method

Cut the bread into thick slices and put some olive oil on the bread and season. Cook in a hot oven for 10 minutes. Roughly chop the tomatoes. In a large bowl, mix the tomatoes, onions, basil and garlic together. Put the mixture on the bread. Mix together the lemon juice and olive oil and drizzle over the top. Season with salt and pepper.

Recipe Background

Whilst out at an Italian restaurant, mum and I chose the Bruschetta as a starter and I was hooked! You wouldn't believe from the above recipe that I wasn't a great fan of tomatoes! This makes a really attractive and colourful plate.

Polpettes

Submitted by Daphne Donnelly, Blackthorn

500 g potatoes
115 g feta cheese
4 spring onions (chopped)
3 tbsp chopped fresh dill
1 beaten egg

1 tbsp lemon juice
Salt and pepper
Flour
3 tbsp olive oil

Cook on hob
Saucepan
Large bowl

Method

Boil the potatoes in their skins, in lightly salted water, until soft.
Drain and peel while warm, place in a bowl and mash. Crumble
the feta cheese into the potatoes and add the spring onions,
dill, egg and lemon juice and season with salt and pepper (not
too much salt as the cheese is already salty), stir well. Cover
the mixture and chill until firm. Divide it into small balls, then
flatten them slightly (looking like a small hamburger). Dip in
flour. Heat the oil in a frying pan and fry the polpettes until
golden brown on each side.

Drain on kitchen towel and serve at once. Goes well with a nice green salad.

Recipe Background

Delicious little fried morsels of potato and Greek feta cheese, flavoured with dill and lemon juice. In Ireland, when I was small we called these rissoles (without the feta, of course!).

Fisherman's Bake

Submitted by Helen Prince, Friend of Blackthorn

2 oz bacon (chopped)
1 bunch spring onions (thinly sliced)
1½ tbsp flour
½ cup clam juice
Water
1¾ lbs baking potatoes (peeled and cut into cubes)

¾ cup double cream
Salt and pepper
6 oz cooked shrimp (peeled)
¾ pound firm fish (I use rockfish - cut into pieces)
2¼ cups crushed saltine crackers

Preheat oven to 190C
Large saucepan
Baking dish (8 inch square)

Serves 4

Method

In a large saucepan, cook the bacon over a medium heat until crisp, and using a slotted spoon, transfer to a bowl. Add the spring onions to the pot and cook until softened. Whisk in the flour and cook, whisking, for 2 minutes. Whisk in the clam juice, and 2 cups water and bring to a boil. Add the potatoes and cook until tender, about 15 minutes. Stir in the cream and season with salt and pepper. In a square baking dish, arrange the

shrimp and then ladle the chowder on top, reserving half a cup.
Top with the fish, season, and pour the remaining chowder on
top. Toss together the crushed crackers and bacon sprinkle on
top. Bake until the fish is cooked through, about 15 minutes.

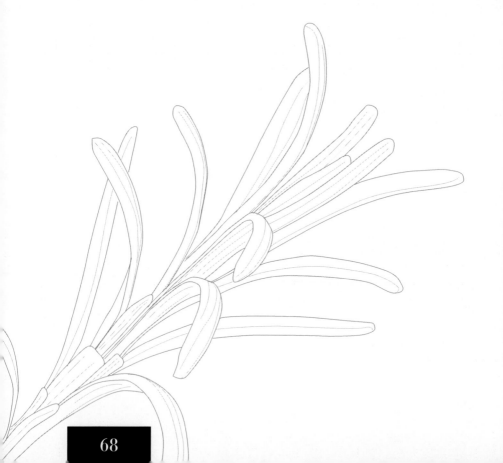

Scottish Pizza

Submitted by Helen Prince, Friend of Blackthorn

3 thin crust pizza bases
Smoked salmon, preferably
Scottish
1 packet of cream cheese
(softened)

1½ tsp white horseradish
Rinsed and drained capers
Dill (fresh is better but can
use dried)

Method

Cook empty pizza bases according to direction. Cool. Mix
softened cream cheese with dill and horseradish. Spread on
pizza, followed by a layer of smoked salmon. Sprinkle capers
and more dill on top. Cut pizza in wedges, serve with lemon
slices.

Pat's Spicy Prawn Linguini

Submitted by Sue and Andy Sparkes, Blackthorn

Good quality linguini or spaghetti (enough for 4)
Generous amount of cooked peeled prawns (enough for 4)
2 tbsp of good olive oil
Zest of 1 lemon
Juice of ½ a lemon
Small glass of white wine

2 cloves of garlic (sliced)
Pinch of sea salt
Pinch of sugar
1 red chilli (chopped and deseeded)
Generous bunch of chopped parsley

Cook on hob
Frying pan
Large saucepan

Serves 4

Method

Heat the oil (but not too hot) and fry the garlic. Add the lemon zest and chilli and turn up the heat. Add the white wine, lemon juice, sugar and salt and heat till bubbling and reduce by a third so the sauce becomes the consistency of a dressing. Take off the heat and leave aside. Cook the pasta for 11 minutes and then drain. Add the prawns to the sauce and reheat. Add to the pasta along with the parsley and toss together. Serve and enjoy.

Optional: cut up some extra chilli for people to sprinkle on their plate for individual spiciness.

Recipe Background

This is a dish created by our brother-in-law Patrick Gillies who is a fantastic cook and has perfected this recipe. It has become a favourite of ours as it is simple, quick and delicious and never fails to excite the taste buds!

Fish Cakes (St Helena)

Submitted by Eileen Masters, Friend of Blackthorn

1 lb fish
1 lb potatoes
1 large onion
(finely chopped)
2 rashers of bacon (finely
chopped - optional)

Chilli (optional)
Pinch of thyme
3 tbsp chopped parsley
1 egg (beaten)
Salt and pepper
Pinch of mixed spice/nutmeg

Cook on hob
Saucepan
Large bowl
Frying pan

Serves 4

Method

Fully cook potatoes in salted water, drain and mash. Place in
a large bowl and leave to cool. Wash fish, shred or mince with
knife until very fine. Heat oil and fry onion, parsley, thyme,
chilli and bacon, until onion starts to brown. Take off heat
and combine with the mashed potato. Add the fish, spices and
beaten egg, mix well. Form patties with your hands, flatten
slightly and dust with flour if necessary. Fry in hot oil until both
sides are brown. Serve as a main meal with rice and vegetables,
or as a snack in a roll.

Seafood Stew with Tomatoes and Basil

Submitted by Margaret Prince, Friend of Blackthorn

¼ cup olive oil
2½ cups crushed tomatoes with added puree
1¼ cups chopped onion
2 tbsp chopped garlic
4 tsp dried oregano
1½ tsp fennel seeds
13-15 oz (2 cans) chopped clams (drained, juice reserved)
1 cup dry white wine

1 lb large shrimp (peeled, deveined - butterflied)
6-8 oz crab meat
1½ lb mussels (scrubbed, beards removed)
1 lb cod fillets (cut into 1 inch pieces)
½ cup chopped fresh basil
2½ cups bottled clam juice
Cayenne, salt, pepper

Cook on hob
Large heavy saucepan

Serves 6

Method

Heat olive oil in pan over medium heat. Add onion, garlic, oregano, and fennel seeds, and sauté until onion is tender, about 8 minutes. Add tomatoes, clam juice, white wine, and liquid reserved from clams. Increase heat and boil until slightly thickened, about 15 minutes. Put mussels in, simmer until the shells open, then remove mussels with tongs and put in a bowl covered with a towel to keep warm. Add clams, shrimp, and cod. Reduce heat and simmer for 2 minutes. Add crab meat. Add basil and simmer for 2 more minutes, season to taste with cayenne, salt and pepper. Now add mussels back into the stew - you will find that most have fallen out of their shells. Put the meat back in along with any 'mussel juice' that drained while they were waiting covered in the bowl. Heat gently for a minute or two. Serve the stew with a green salad and plenty of Italian bread to dip in the sauce!

Smoked Mackerel in a Crimson Dressing

Submitted by June Foreman, Tailor Made Catering Solutions

1 large Bramley apple
½ oz butter
8 oz cooked beetroot
2 tsp creamed horseradish
1 rounded tbsp yoghurt
Seasoning including cider or
wine vinegar and sugar

12 oz smoked mackerel fillets
(skinned)
½ a cucumber
Dill (to garnish)

Cook on hob
Saucepan
Blender
Serving dish or individual plates

Serves 6

Method

Peel, core and slice the apple and cook tightly covered in a
little water until it falls into a puree and beat in the butter. In
a blender puree the beetroot with the apple, horseradish and
yoghurt, season with salt, pepper, sugar and a dash of vinegar.
Allow to cool. Slice the cucumber and arrange slices round
the puree on a serving dish or individual plates. Place sliced
mackerel fillets on top and garnish with dill. Serve with crusty
brown bread and butter.

Seafood Platter

Submitted by Sandie Stevenson, Blackthorn

16 scallops (removed from shell)
12 oysters (frozen or freshly shucked)
Small onion (finely chopped)
2 slices of back bacon (diced)
Mature Cheddar cheese (grated)

3 oz butter
Drop of olive oil
Breadcrumbs
Salt and freshly ground black pepper
Parsley and lemon wedges (to garnish)

Preheat oven to 200C
Cook on hob
Frying pan

Serves 4

Method

For the scallops: melt the butter and add the oil. Gently sauté the onion and add the scallops. Gently brown for 2 minutes, turn once during cooking. When cooked return to shell. For the oysters: fry the diced bacon and place a little on each oyster. Sprinkle over the grated cheese and breadcrumbs and bake in a preheated oven for 15 minutes, or until golden brown. Plate up the scallops and baked oysters and garnish with parsley and lemon wedges. Makes a great meal and is ready in a flash.

Thai Fish Cakes (Thod Mun Pla) with Cucumber Relish

Submitted by Sue and Andy Sparkes, Blackthorn

550 g white fish (minced)
1 egg
½ cup snake beans/green beans (finely sliced)
10 kaffir lime leaves (finely chopped)
1 tsp sugar
1 tsp salt

1 tbsp red chilli paste
Cooking oil (for frying)
1 cup of diced cucumber
½ cup sugar
½ cup white wine vinegar/rice wine vinegar
½ cup of diced red onion

Cook on hob
Food processor
Pan suitable for deep frying
Small saucepan

Makes approximately 20

Method

Mince the fish in a processor then put with all the ingredients in a large bowl and mix well by hand until thoroughly combined. Shape approximately 2 tbsp at a time into small patties of about 3 inch diameter. Allow to rest in the fridge for approximately 30 minutes. Deep fry in hot oil until golden brown.
For the cucumber relish: Put the sugar and vinegar in a pan

and heat on the hob until it comes to the boil and the sugar has completely dissolved. Remove from the heat and allow to cool. Add cucumber and red onion. Chill before serving with fish cakes.

Parmesan Salmon

Submitted by Christine Neville, Friend of Blackthorn

4 fillets of salmon
Butter
Parmesan cheese

Preheat oven to 200C   Serves 4
Baking tray

Method

Brush fillets of salmon with a little melted butter. Top each one
with a tbsp of grated Parmesan cheese and bake in the oven for
10-15 minutes until golden and the salmon is cooked. Serve
with sun dried red pepper sauce and a selection of cooked
vegetables.

Smoked Salmon Pasta

Submitted by Daphne Donnelly, Blackthorn

4 ripe tomatoes
1 small onion
Olive oil
Tomato puree (dash)
Pinch of salt, pepper,
oregano and marjoram

1 cup of white wine/water
4 good slices of smoked
salmon (chopped)
Handful of frozen peas
Large tbsp of crème fraiche

Cook on hob
Large frying pan

Serves 2-4

Method

Fry the onion and tomatoes gently in the olive oil for a few
minutes until the tomatoes and onions have softened. Add the
white wine or water (depending on your taste), tomato puree
and seasonings. Cook for about 10-15 minutes until it is slightly
thickened. Add a little more water or wine if it reduces too
much. Add the chopped smoked salmon and the small handful
of peas and cook for about 5 minutes. Just before you are ready
to serve, add the crème fraiche and heat gently for a couple of
minutes. Serve with any pasta of your choice.

Top Tip

As an alternative to cooking the tomato sauce yourself, an excellent substitute is a sachet of sun-ripened tomato and basil sauce. Use this and just follow the recipe from where you add the smoked salmon.

No time to cook? This is ideal for a quick meal when a friend pops around. 15-20 minutes and it is ready.

Watercress Chicken

Submitted by Naomi Karslake, Blackthorn

4 chicken breasts
100 g light mayonnaise

100 g light fromage frais
100 g washed watercress

Preheat oven to 170C
Ovenproof dish
Liquidiser

Serves 8

Method

Poach the chicken in a moderate oven for 40 minutes until cooked through and leave to cool. Put a small amount of the watercress on one side. Place the mayonnaise, fromage frais and rest of the watercress in the liquidiser and liquidise until almost smooth. Place the chicken on a plate, pour one quarter of the sauce over each one and garnish with the remaining watercress. Serve with boiled new potatoes and salad of rocket and baby tomatoes

Recipe Background

We invented this recipe the summer of 2003 when the weather was always glorious and we had endless lunches in the garden to celebrate important birthdays.

Stir-fried Chicken with Ginger

Submitted by Tracie Gilllies, Friend of Blackthorn

3 tbsp olive oil
1 tbsp chopped garlic
2 cups of chicken (cut into
bite-sized pieces)
1 cup sliced mushrooms
½ cup rat ear mushrooms
(soaked in water and drained)
5 shitake mushrooms
(soaked, drained and sliced)
2 tbsp oyster sauce

½ tbsp palm sugar
3 tbsp chopped onion
4 inch piece of root ginger
(cut into fine strips)
2 red chillies (jalapeno)
½ cup of chopped spring
onion
4 tbsp soy sauce
1 tbsp fish sauce

Cook on hob
Wok

Method

Mix fish sauce, soy sauce and oyster sauce and set aside. Bring oil to smoking point in a wok. Add chicken and garlic and stir until the chicken begins to change colour. Add mixed sauces and sugar. Stir until chicken is cooked through, approximately 5 minutes. Add remaining ingredients and stir for 1 minute, then serve.

Country Chicken Casserole

Submitted by June Foreman, Tailor Made Catering Solutions

6 chicken breasts
2 oz seasoned flour
2 oz butter
8 small onions
3 sticks celery
1 pt chicken stock
1 lemon (sliced)
1 bay leaf
4-6 oz carrots

4 oz frozen peas
¼ pt of sour cream/crème fraiche
For the dumplings:
4 oz self raising flour
½ tsp salt
1½ oz shredded suet
½ tsp oregano/marjoram
1 tbsp tomato puree

Preheat oven to 180C
Large frying pan
Casserole dish

Serves 6-8

Method

Cut the chicken into pieces and toss in seasoned flour. Heat butter and fry chicken until golden and put into a casserole dish. Fry onions, carrots and celery and add to chicken. Stir any flour remaining into fat in pan and gradually add stock, bring to the boil and stir until thickened. Pour over chicken. Add lemon and bay leaf. Cover and cook for about 45 minutes. Remove lemon slices.

To make dumplings: sieve flour and salt, add suet, herbs and tomato puree. Make a soft dough with water. Form into balls and cook in boiling salted water or stock for about 20 minutes. Add to casserole with frozen peas and soured cream and pop back into the oven for a few minutes then serve with potatoes and vegetables of your choice.

Chicken Enchiladas

Submitted by Nicola Leggett, Friend of Blackthorn

2 chicken breast fillets
1 pepper (sliced)
1 onion (chopped)
1 carrot (sliced thinly)
1 tsp oregano
2 tsp chilli powder

1 tsp cumin
100 g cheese
1 tin of tomatoes (drained)
Tortilla wraps (4 or 6)
1 tbsp oil

Preheat oven to 200C
Large frying pan

Serves 4-6

Method

Pour oil into large pan and shallow fry chicken for 5 minutes.
Add onion, cook until soft. Add pepper and carrot and cook for
5 minutes. Add oregano, chilli and cumin, cook for 2 minutes.
Add drained tomatoes and cook for a further minute. Add
cheese and stir. Place mixture in tortilla wraps to form parcels,
wrap in tin foil. Put in oven and bake for 35 minutes. Serve with
guacamole, yoghurt and salsa, plus a side salad.

Chicken and Smoked Bacon Lasagne

Submitted by Tessa, Friend of Blackthorn

8 chicken breasts
8 rashers smoked streaky bacon
2 oz butter
2 tbsp sunflower oil
1 onion (finely chopped)
1-2 cloves of garlic (very finely chopped)

8 oz mushrooms (wiped and chopped)
2 oz flour
2 pts milk
Salt and ground black pepper
12 sheets green lasagne
3 oz grated Cheddar cheese

Preheat oven to 180C
Food processor
Wide saucepan
Large ovenproof dish

Serves 6

Method

Slice chicken into bits, removing skin and bones. Cut bacon into 1 inch lengths. Put the chicken in the food processor with the bacon. Whiz together for a quick burst just to chop. Heat the oil and melt the butter together in a wide saucepan and brown chicken mixture, using a wooden spoon to break it up. Put in a warm dish. Cook onion and garlic until soft and just beginning to turn brown. Add the mushrooms and immediately stir in the flour. Gradually add the milk, stirring all the time until the sauce boils. Take the pan off the heat and stir in the chicken mixture, season with the salt and pepper. Spoon some of the sauce over the base of a buttered ovenproof dish. Cover with a layer of lasagne, and then cover with more sauce. Continue layering, finishing off with the sauce. Scatter the grated cheese over the surface. Bake for about 30 minutes, until the pasta in the middle is soft and the cheese is golden brown. Serve as soon as possible.

Chicken in Cider

Submitted by Virginie Halphen, Blackthorn

1 chicken (cut into pieces)
6 apples
30 cl dry cider
20 g of butter

15 cl thick cream
Nutmeg
Salt and pepper

Cook on hob
Casserole dish

Serves 6

Method

Melt the butter in a casserole dish and brown the pieces of
chicken. Season with salt and pepper and pour in the cider.
Cover the casserole dish and cook gently over a slow heat for
45 minutes. Peel the apples and cut them into thick slices.
Incorporate the cream to the cooking juice then add the apples
and a little grated nutmeg. Cook for a further 20 minutes. Serve
very hot.

Recipe Background

This is an old recipe from Brittany, but of course you can use
Blackthorn cider to make this delicious dish! You can replace
the whole chicken with chicken breasts, but check the timings.

Recipe Background

I first cooked this
dish as part of a PTA
fund-raising dinner.
A small group of us
had to cook this dish
for 80 people! It was a
great success and has
now become a family
favourite.

Chicken Meyer

Submitted by Anne Lee, Blackthorn

4 chicken breasts
1 lb broccoli
1 tin of condensed chicken
soup (small)

4 tbsp mayonnaise
4 tbsp single cream
3 tsp curry powder (medium)
Grated cheese

Preheat oven to 180C
Large saucepan
Large ovenproof dish
Mixing bowl

Serves 4

Method

Separate broccoli into segments and put into boiling water
for 2-3 minutes. Remove, drain and put in bottom of large
ovenproof dish. Put chicken breasts on top. Mix cream,
mayonnaise, soup and curry powder together and pour over the
chicken and broccoli. Put grated cheese on top. Bake for about
45 minutes (until chicken is cooked). Serve with potato wedges
or new potatoes.

Grandma's Chicken Pie

Submitted by Teresa Bannock, Blackthorn

2 packets of ready made puff pastry

8 chicken breasts

1 small onion (chopped)

½ small packet of sage and onion stuffing mix

1 tbsp Worcestershire sauce

Beaten egg and milk (to glaze)

Preheat oven to 180C

Large saucepan

Baking tray

Serves 8

Method

Chop chicken breasts into regular sized pieces and place in saucepan. Add chopped onion. Cover with boiling water and simmer for 10–15 minutes until chicken is cooked. Drain chicken and onion (the stock from this can be used to make chicken soup). Unroll 1 pack of puff pastry and place on a greased baking tray. Sprinkle sage and onion stuffing mix evenly over pastry leaving approximately ½ inch around the edge. Sprinkle Worcestershire sauce over the stuffing mix. Spread cooked chicken and onion over the stuffing mix. Brush ½ inch gap with egg and milk mixture. Unroll second pack of puff pastry and place over the top of the chicken and pinch to seal with the bottom layer. Make a small hole in the centre of the pie and then brush all over with egg/milk to glaze. Bake in the oven for 40 minutes until golden brown.

Recipe Background

This is another approximation of a dish my mother-in-law used to make for the family. It was usually accompanied by chicken soup made from the stock from cooking the chicken (she usually used a whole chicken and then divested it of all the flesh, but using chicken breasts is easier).

Thai Red Chicken Curry

Submitted by Tracie Gillies, Friend of Blackthorn

Thai red chilli paste
(homemade):
2 red onions (chopped)
8-10 medium red chillies
(chopped)
2 lemon grass bulbs
10 kaffir lime leaves
2 heads garlic (20 cloves)
4 inch galangal root
(chopped)
1 tsp shrimp paste
Handful coriander root

1-1.5kg of chicken legs
Vegetable oil
2 cans coconut milk
2 Thai purple aubergines
(roughly chopped)
4-5 crispy Thai aubergines
(roughly chopped)
Handful of aubergine peas
Handful of French beans
(trimmed and cut in half)
1 tin bamboo shoots
½ pt chicken stock

Cook on hob
Blender
Large saucepan

Serves 4

Method

For the paste: Put all the paste ingredients into a blender/mixer and pulse until well blended, but not smooth. If too thick add a splash of olive oil and blend until looser. Put paste to one side.

Cook chicken, allow to cool then remove from the bone. Heat a couple of tablespoons of vegetable oil in a large pan. Add 3 tbsp of red chilli paste and fry until deep red (5 minutes) add the chicken meat and stir. Add the 2 cans of coconut milk and add the chicken stock. Bring up to a fast simmer. Add the vegetables and bring up to heat. Season to taste with fish sauce, soy sauce and sugar. Cook through for 5 minutes. Serve strewn with whole sweet Thai basil leaves.

Top Tip

The ingredients for the chilli paste will make double the quantity you require so you can freeze the rest for next time.

Swiss Chicken

Submitted by Odette Buckle, Friend of Blackthorn

4 chicken breasts
Salt and pepper (to season)
1 tbsp flour
3 oz butter
1 garlic clove (crushed)
¾ cup of dry white wine

1 tsp French mustard
½ cup of cream
3 shallots/small onions (finely sliced)
8 slices of ham
8 slices of Swiss cheese

Cook on hob
Preheat oven to 160C
Frying pan with lid
Ovenproof dish

Method

Slice the chicken breasts in half so you have 8 pieces. Dust the chicken breasts lightly with flour and season with salt and pepper. Heat the butter and crushed garlic. Put chicken into pan and brown lightly. Add the wine and bring to the boil, then reduce the heat till gently simmering. Cover for 20 minutes or until the chicken is tender. Remove from the pan (keep reduced liquid) and wrap each piece in ham and top with a slice of cheese. Put in a dish and cook for 10 minutes, until the cheese has melted. While the chicken is in the oven bring the liquid in the pan back up to the boil, until there is about half a cup full left. Reduce the heat and add the shallots and mustard and cream and season to taste. Pour the cream sauce over the cooked chicken and serve with vegetables of your choice.

Chicken in Curry and Lemon

Submitted by Judith Wood, Blackthorn

6 chicken breasts
1½ oz flour
2 tsp curry powder
2 oz butter
¾ pt chicken stock
3 small onions (chopped)

1 lemon (thinly sliced)
2 bay leaves
2 tbsp olive oil
Toasted almonds and
chopped parsley (to garnish)

Preheat oven to 180C
Large frying pan
Ovenproof casserole dish
(Or do the whole lot in a cast iron dish to save washing up!)

Serves 8

Method

Mix curry powder and flour in a bag and toss chicken breasts in the mixture to coat them. Melt butter and oil together and fry coated chicken until golden brown on all sides (10–15 minutes). Remove from pan and put to one side. Fry onions in same pan for 5 minutes. Add remaining curry powder and flour and cook for a further minute. Stir in stock, lemon slices and bay leaves. Bring to the boil, stirring all the time. Put chicken and sauce in ovenproof dish. Cover and cook for 1 hour.

Garnish with almonds and parsley before serving. Freezes well.

Recipe Background

A friend who introduced me to my husband gave me this recipe when I asked for something foolproof that I could cook for him. We've just celebrated our silver wedding anniversary, and I still cook it regularly!

Thousand Island Chicken

Submitted by Missy Fetterolf, Blackthorn

4-6 large boneless chicken breasts
1 packet onion soup mix
1 jar apricot jam

Equal parts water and salad dressing
(Mayo, sweet relish and ketchup)

Preheat oven to 180C
Large frying pan

Method

Mix all the ingredients and pour over the chicken. Bake for 1 hour and 30 minutes, or until chicken is cooked and the sauce has started to caramelise. Serve over boiled white rice.

Recipe Background

This recipe comes all the way from America via Moscow.

Main Courses
- Meat & Game

Country Casserole

Submitted by Tessa, Friend of Blackthorn

1 lb pork sausage meat
1-2 tbsp seasoned flour
2 tbsp oil
Onion Sauce:
1 oz butter
2 onions (peeled and finely chopped)
1 oz plain flour

½ pt milk (or mixture of milk and chicken stock)
Salt and pepper
1 lb 13 oz seasoned creamed potatoes
2 oz grated strong Cheddar cheese
Sprig of fresh sage (garnish)

Preheat oven to 180C
Large frying pan
Deep casserole dish
Small saucepan

Serves 8

Method

Divide sausage meat into 8 patties and lightly coat with seasoned flour. Heat the oil in a large frying pan and cook the patties gently on each side until lightly coloured, drain and arrange in a deep casserole. To make the onion sauce, melt the butter in a small pan and add the onions. Cook gently until soft but not coloured. Stir in the flour and cook for 2 minutes. Gradually add the milk, stirring constantly, then bring to the boil and simmer for 10 minutes. Season to taste. Pour over the meat, cover and bake for 45 minutes. Remove casserole dish from oven, uncover and pipe or spoon creamed potato over the top, right to the edge. Sprinkle with the cheese. Raise oven temperature to 200C and replace the uncovered casserole for about 20 minutes, or until golden brown. Garnish with sage.

Osso Buco alla Milanese

Submitted by Missy Fetterolf, Blackthorn

4 thick slices of veal (with a piece of marrow bone)
Flour
50 g butter
125 ml dry white wine
8 oz tomatoes (peeled and chopped)
Meat stock/water

Salt and pepper
4 tbsp of finely chopped parsley
1 tbsp of finely grated lemon rind
1 small clove of garlic (crushed)
1 anchovy (finely chopped)

Cook on hob
Large saucepan

Serves 4

Method

Coat the meat with flour and brown in butter on both sides.
Add the wine and simmer for 10 minutes. Add the tomatoes
and stock or water to cover. Season. Cook with the lid on for
1½–2 hours stirring occasionally to make sure it does not stick
and until the meat is so tender it comes away from the bone.
Add stock or water to keep the meat covered at first. The sauce
should be thick at the end. Make what is called a 'gremolata': a
mixture of parsley, grated lemon rind and garlic (and anchovy
if you like). Place a little on each piece of meat and cook a few
minutes longer. Buon Appetito!

Risotto alla Milanese

This is the traditional partner to Osso Buco alla Milanese

Submitted by Missy Fetterolf, Blackthorn

1 small onion (chopped)
Small piece of marrow from
a beef bone (optional)
50 g butter
1 ltr of mushroom stock

125 ml dry white/red wine
275 g Arborio rice
Salt
1 envelope of saffron powder
50 g Parmesan (grated)

Cook on hob
Large frying pan
Medium saucepan

Serves 4

Method

In a large pan fry the onion and marrow in half the butter until soft. In a separate pan heat the stock. Add the wine to the fried onion and boil until much reduced. Add the rice and stir to coat the grains well. Add salt and the boiling stock by the ladleful stirring all the time as it becomes absorbed. Add the saffron towards the end. When the rice is done there should be enough liquid to make it creamy, but the grains must still be firm. Add the rest of the butter and the Parmesan.

Pheasant with Green Apples

Submitted by Becca, Dan and Moley, Blackthorn

1 Pheasant
¼ lb bacon (diced)
½ Spanish onion (finely chopped)
1 garlic clove (finely chopped)

2 tbsp butter
2 tbsp olive oil
4 small cooking apples
4 tbsp Cointreau
½ pt cream
Salt and pepper

Preheat oven to 140C
Ovenproof casserole dish
Blender

Serves 2

Method

Gently fry the bacon, onion and garlic in oil and butter in a casserole dish until brown. Remove and reserve. Brown the pheasant on all sides in the remaining fat, remove and keep warm. Peel, core and slice the apples thickly and fry them in the same remaining fat until they turn golden. At this point pour over the Cointreau. Remove apples from the casserole. Skim the fat and return pheasant to the dish surrounding it with the apples, bacon, onions and garlic. Cover and allow to simmer for 10 minutes or so. Stir in the cream and cook in the oven until pheasant is tender. When done remove bacon bits and pheasant to a clean dish and keep warm. Place the sauce and apples into a blender and puree. Correct the seasoning, re-heat the sauce and pour over the pheasant. Serve straight away with a green veg and game chips (ready salted crisps will do).

Recipe Background

A great favourite and ideal when there is a surplus of apples from the garden. This sauce can be made leaving out the bacon bits - freeze it as it goes well with pork too.

Fool Proof Rib Roast

Submitted by Helen Prince, Friend of Blackthorn

1 rib roast, any size, (must be
at room temperature)
Salt, pepper, or any seasoning
you desire

Start the process below about 6 hours before you want to serve
the meat!

Preheat oven to 190C
Roasting pan

Method

Rub roast with seasonings. Place in open roasting pan, rib side
down, on a rack. Roast for 1 hour then turn off oven. DO NOT
OPEN THE OVEN DOOR AT ANY TIME! I tape the oven
door with a note to warn my family not to open the door as this
is all important. 30-40 minutes before dinner turn on the oven
again (same temperature) for the final re-heating. Regardless of
the size of your roast it will be well browned outside and rare
inside. If you like it less rare, just add more time to the final
re-heating. The secret to the success is the closed oven door and
the room temperature roast!

South African Bobotie

Submitted by Georgina Lamb, Friend of Blackthorn

15 g butter/1 tbsp oil
2 medium onions (chopped)
2 cloves of garlic (chopped)
1 kg minced beef/lamb
1½ tbsp mild curry powder
½ tbsp sugar
4 tbsp lemon juice

50 g flaked almonds
150 g raisins
Salt and pepper
2 thick slices of bread (100 g approx)
2 eggs
250 ml milk

Preheat oven to 180C
Frying pan
Ovenproof dish

Serves 4-6

Method

Gently fry together the onions, garlic and mince in the butter. Mix together the curry powder, sugar, lemon juice, almonds and raisins, season with salt and pepper. Add to the onion mixture. Put in dish and place bread on top. Beat together eggs and milk and pour over the bread. Bake in the oven for 45-50 minutes until top is set and brown.

Chopstick Steak

Submitted by Alex Grell, Blackthorn

About 2 lb good quality steak meat (sirloin or rump – needs to be big/thick enough to be cut in 1 inch cubes)
A little rapeseed oil (for frying the beef)
2 tbsp finely chopped ginger
¼ cup chopped spring onions
¼ cup chopped chives
¼ cup chopped celery
¼ cup watercress

Slightly less than ¼ cup chopped fresh basil and mint leaves
(This also works nicely with other vegetables in season, like radish, leek, flat leaf parsley etc)
¼ cup dashi
¼ cup soy sauce
Splash rice vinegar

Cook on hob
Pan/wok for frying

Serves 4-6

Method

Dashi shoyu sauce: Combine ¼ cup dashi with ¼ cup soy sauce and add a splash of rice vinegar. Heat (don't boil) and then leave to cool down completely. Fry the cubes of steak in the rapeseed oil over a good heat, turning frequently so that all sides are brown and the cubes are cooked to your liking – place on a serving dish. Mix together the vegetables and sprinkle over the meat cubes. Pour the cooled dashi soy sauce over the meat and vegetables and serve. This is a great way to enjoy steak. It is light, tasty, and seasonal – and looks great!

Recipe Background

I came across this way of preparing beef in Japan, where we used to live for quite some time before coming to Blackthorn. Freshness, flavour, texture and presentation are what Japanese cuisine is known for all over the world but there is something else at the heart of Japanese cuisine that is not as well known: seasonality. Great importance is placed on not only eating vegetables seasonally, they are also prepared and presented in ways to celebrate the seasons. In Japan, I used the famous Kobe beef for this dish, but any good quality cut will produce the same results because it is the way the flavours and textures of the meat and the crunchy, raw vegetables play against and with each other that makes this dish so exciting. The recipe above is obviously altered from the Japanese one as it uses English vegetables but they work just as well. The only thing you need to use as per the original Japanese recipe is an ingredient called dashi (easy to find instant dashi on the internet); a stock made from kombu (dried kelp) and dried tuna flakes.

Beef Stew

Submitted by Teresa Bannock, Blackthorn

1 lb stewing steak
2 medium carrots
1 parsnip
½ swede
2 medium potatoes
½ savoy cabbage
1 medium onion

1 tin of chopped tomatoes
1 oz pearl barley
1 packet dried oxtail
soup mix
3 ltr beef/vegetable stock
1 tbsp oil

Cook on hob
Large stock pot

Serves 6

Method

Chop all vegetables into regular size cubes. Cut beef into small pieces, discarding any fat, and brown in the oil in a large stock pot. Place all remaining ingredients except cabbage into the stock pot and bring to the boil. Simmer gently for at least 1 hour until vegetables have softened. Add cabbage and simmer for a further 15-20 minutes. This stew gets better the longer you cook it for. It also benefits from the addition of suet dumplings. Serve in large bowls with plenty of bread for dipping.

Recipe Background

When I was a child my father (who never usually cooked)
would make this in a very large stock pot with vegetables that
he had grown in the garden. He always used 'Chefs Square
Shaped Soups' oxtail soup mix, which gave it a very distinct
flavour. You can put almost any vegetables in this stew. I have
tried mushrooms, leeks and peas amongst other more exotic
ingredients. You can also replace the beef with chicken or lamb.

Sheila's Meatballs

Submitted by Jenny Thompson, Blackthorn

Meatballs:
500 g minced beef
1 medium onion (finely
chopped)
1 egg
1 Oxo cube (crumbled)
Worcestershire sauce (to
taste)
Salt and pepper
Knob of butter/olive oil (to
fry with)

Sauce:
1 medium onion (finely
chopped)
2 oz (more if you like)
chopped mushrooms
½ pint of stock (using 1 beef
Oxo cube and 1 beef Knorr
cube)
2 tbsp tomato puree
1 garlic clove (crushed)
2 tsp of sugar
Pepper

Preheat oven to 170C
Large greased ovenproof dish
Mixing bowl
Frying pan

Serves 2-3

Method

For meatballs: fry onion gently until soft. Mix meat, onion, egg,
crumbled Oxo cube, Worcestershire sauce, few turns of salt and
pepper in a bowl. Using floured hands make into 4 or 6 flatish

balls! In the same pan fry over medium heat until browned on both sides. Put into greased ovenproof dish.

For the sauce: fry onion gently until soft. Add mushrooms and garlic, then mix in tomato puree. Make up stock and add sugar and pepper (usually already has sufficient salt due to the stock cubes) and pour over the meatballs. Cook for roughly 1 hour, then turn heat down until ready to eat. The sauce should have reduced a little and the meatballs slightly browned on top. If getting too brown, continue cooking covered with tin foil. Can be made a day in advance and reheats really well. Serve with mashed spuds and green veggies......or whatever you feel like. Good winter fodder!

Recipe Background

This is an oft requested meal when we go to see Betty, my mother-in-law (the name of the dish simply comes from a friend of hers who passed it on years ago). It's a hearty winter comfort food that is full of taste and goes especially well with mash or slightly cut up well buttered new spuds. Try making with 650 g to 700 g of mince so that 8 balls can be made and can therefore be warmed up for a second night - 2 balls each night for 2 people!

Mrs Plank's Pot Roast

Submitted by Sandie Stevenson, Blackthorn

Oil (for frying)
3 lb of good quality red meat
(roasting joint)
Salt and pepper
½ pt beef stock (made with
water and Oxo cube)

½ a bottle of red wine
(optional)
2 cloves of garlic (optional)
4 whole small onions
4 whole carrots

Cook on hob
Preheat oven to 180C
2 large saucepans
Large casserole dish

Method

Fry the joint and brown on all sides. Place all the other
ingredients into another pan and bring to the boil. Transfer
to a casserole dish, add the joint and cook in the oven for
40 minutes. Increase heat to 200C and cook for a further 20
minutes. Serve with roast potatoes, Yorkshire puddings and any
green veg.

Truckers' Pie

Submitted by Teresa Bannock, Blackthorn

1 lb minced beef
1 small onion (finely chopped)
1 small tin of tomato puree
1 tin of baked beans
8 oz plain flour
4 oz butter/good margarine

2 oz rolled oats (optional)
4 oz grated strong cheese (normally Cheddar but can vary according to personal taste)
1 tbsp Worcestershire sauce

Preheat oven to 180C
Frying pan
Mixing bowl
Baking or casserole dish

Serves 6

Method

Brown the mince and onion in a pan, mixing them together as you go. Drain off any excess fat. Add the tomato puree, baked beans and Worcestershire sauce. Combine thoroughly and heat gently until bubbling. Separately rub flour and butter together until the mixture resembles breadcrumbs. Add the grated cheese and oats (if required) and stir gently with a spoon to combine. Place the meat mixture into an appropriate sized baking or casserole dish. Cover with the crumble mix. Bake for

40 minutes or until a pale golden brown.

Recipe Background

This is a recipe I cobbled together after my husband described
something his mum used to make when he was a small boy.
My children love this and it is so easy to make from items you
probably already have at home. You can vary the ingredients to
suit your own taste making it hot and spicy or veggie if you like.

Beef Goulash

Submitted by Ruth Harris, Friend of Blackthorn

50 g lard/oil
1 kg chuck steak
350 g onions (peeled and thinly sliced)
1 green pepper
1 tbsp flour
1 tbsp paprika

2 tbsp of tomato puree
Salt and freshly ground black pepper
½ pt of beef stock
½ pt sour cream
1 tbsp parsley (finely chopped)

Preheat oven to 160C
Cook on the hob first, and then move to a preheated oven
Frying pan
Casserole dish

Method

Heat oil in pan, add meat and fry briskly till browned. Remove and put in casserole dish. Reduce heat and add onions and green pepper and fry till soft. Sprinkle in flour and paprika and cook for 1 minute. Stir in puree and seasoning; gradually add stock and bring to boil stirring constantly. Pour sauce over meat and cover casserole dish. Cook for 2 hours 30 minutes (or until tender). Just before serving stir in soured cream and sprinkle with chopped parsley (you might want to serve soured cream separately).

Spaghetti Bolognese

Submitted by C W Mobbs, Blackthorn

3-4 cloves of garlic
1 large onion
3-4 flat mushrooms
500 g mince
1 x 400 g tin of chopped
tomatoes
1 jar of tomato based sauce
Dash of olive oil
Knob of butter
1 beef stock cube

Italian herb seasoning and
oregano (to taste)
Salt and pepper (to taste)
Minimum 75 g spaghetti,
fettuccine or linguine per
person
Grated mozzarella and
Cheddar cheese
Freshly ground black pepper

Preheat oven to 120C
Large frying pan
Large oven proof dish
Large saucepan

Serves 2-5

Method

Peel garlic, onion and mushrooms and slice. Place onion and
garlic in frying pan with butter and olive oil and sauté until soft.
Remove from pan. Sauté and brown mushrooms and remove
from pan and place with garlic and onion. Brown mince in frying
pan, drain excess water and add garlic, onions, mushrooms,

chopped tomatoes, bolognese sauce, stock cube, herbs and salt and pepper. Stir and bring to the boil and when boiling, place in oven to simmer for approximately one hour. 15 minutes before serving time, bring a pan of water to the boil, add selected pasta and cook until tender, and then drain. Serve with grated cheese, black pepper and garlic bread.

Recipe Background

I have found that bought spaghetti bolognese is always unsatisfying as a meal. This one is bulked up with the addition of mushrooms, onions and chopped tomatoes and is therefore more fulfilling. Furthermore, it forms a useful base for additional meals.

Beef,Ginger and Chilli Stir-fry

Submitted by The Andersons, Blackthorn

500 g rump/sirloin steak
3-4 bird's eye chillies
(according to taste)
3-4 large garlic cloves
Large piece of root ginger
1 dsp of brown sugar

Thai soy sauce (enough to
cover but not soak)
1-2 bunches of spring onions
2 red peppers
Handful of mange tout
Coriander bunch

Cook on hob
Wok

Serves 4

The meat needs to marinate for at least 6 hours (preferably overnight).

Method

Finely chop chilli, crush garlic, peel then finely slice or grate ginger. Place in a medium sized freezer bag and add whole steak with sugar and soy. Seal bag and place in fridge to marinate. One hour before cooking remove steak from bag leaving other ingredients still in bag. Remove fat from steak and slice into 5 cm strips. Return meat to bag. Finely slice pepper and spring onions. Chop coriander leaves. Put wok on high heat – with vegetable oil to thinly cover wok. When hot add contents of freezer bag and cook for 2-3 minutes. Add spring onions and peppers and cook for a further 2-3 minutes. Finally add mange tout and coriander. Serve with sticky Thai rice or noodles (cook as per manufacturer's instructions).

Recipe background

We love Thai food and 'invented' this dish whilst living in Blackthorn. Hope you like it too.

Brassato

Submitted by Daphne Donnelly, Blackthorn

2½ lb topside beef
1-2 slices of smoked bacon
(streaky)
1 small onion
2 garlic cloves

2 tbsp olive oil
1 sachet of bouquet garni
1 carrot (sliced lengthways)
½ bottle of red wine
Salt and pepper

Cook on hob
Frying pan
Casserole dish

Serves 6

Method

Chop or puree the garlic cloves. Chop the bacon into very tiny pieces. With a very long thin knife, insert it into the beef and turn it around making a long bore hole. Put pieces of the garlic and the bacon into the hole. Continue to make incisions all around the meat, stuffing it with the garlic and bacon. If you have the time, wrap the meat in cling film and let it marinate overnight. Brown and seal the meat in the olive oil in a frying pan. Put to the side to rest. Chop the onion very finely and fry in the remaining oil in the pan. Add the red wine and bring to the boil. Salt and pepper according to taste. Put the joint of beef in a casserole dish together with the carrot, red wine and the bouquet garni and cover. Cook for approximately 1½ to 2 hours depending on the size of the joint. When cooked, the meat will be extremely tender and easy to carve. Thicken the gravy; I use cornflour or gravy granules. Serve with your choice of vegetables and potatoes.

Recipe Background

This is a favourite from Dan's Italian Mum.

Medallions of Sirloin Beef with Rosti Potatoes

Submitted by Ruth and Tim Harvey, Blackthorn

2 large baking potatoes
2 tsp paprika
Oil for (frying)
700 g sirloin beef (trimmed
into medallions - 2 each)

4 shallots
150 ml white wine
300 ml double cream
2 dsp horseradish sauce
Salt and pepper

Cook on hob
Frying pans

Method

Peel and grate the potatoes. Season well. Put into a tea towel
and squeeze over a sink to extract water. Season again and add
paprika. Squash into balls and press down (so they look like
thick biscuits, they don't have to look perfect). Heat oil in frying
pan until smoking. Cook for at least 5 minutes until potato starts
to brown then turn over. When brown put them on cooling rack
until needed (they can be made much earlier in day). When
needed just pop in oven for 10 minutes. Sear medallions in hot
pan (or on griddle) for a couple of minutes each side. Remove
and allow to rest. When needed just pop in oven for 6 minutes.

For the sauce: chop and sweat shallots in a little oil then add wine and reduce (this can be done in advance). Add cream and horseradish and reduce again. Taste, season and it's ready when it coats the back of a spoon.

To serve: put warm rosti in middle of plate, top with beef and pour sauce around and over. You can serve with cabbage and baby vegetables or mange tout and carrots.

Top Tip

This may sound complicated but it's really very easy, just do everything you can in advance and then you're ready for the main event.......... pudding!

Bob the Gardener's Saturday Evening Chilli

Submitted by Bob Massingham, Friend of Blackthorn

1 lb of lean minced beef
Tin of tomatoes
Tin of kidney beans
1 onion (finely chopped)
1 clove garlic (finely chopped)
½ tsp cumin seeds (crushed)
1 tbsp flour
Salt and pepper

1 tsp (variable according to taste) Very Lazy Chillies
Beef dripping (this gives it much more flavour than olive oil or a 'light' oil)
A green capsicum (optional)
Soured cream/crème fraiche
3 oz white rice (per person)

Cook on hob
Cast iron casserole dish with lid
Saucepan with lid

Serves 4

Method

Heat the casserole dish and melt the beef dripping – not too hot at this stage. Add the onion, garlic and crushed cumin seeds and cook the onions until translucent. Turn the heat up and put the mince in the pot, keep it moving until evenly brown and cooked through. Add the flour and stir in, next add the tin of kidney beans (minus the fluid) and the tin of tomatoes. Add salt and pepper – plenty of both works for me. Now the tricky bit, add 1 level tsp of chillies (I'm a big fan of these – but fresh chillies will obviously work superbly) you can always add more, but adjust the dose of chillies to your taste. Cook over a low flame on the hob for 45 minutes with the lid on or put in a moderate preheated oven for an hour. About half way through either method you can add the chopped green pepper - it adds a nice colour and texture. Cook rice, as recommended on the packet, usually 10-12 minutes. Serve up on heated plates and add a dollop of soured cream/crème fraiche.

Top Tip

You can mix and match this with tortilla chips and salsa. This goes well with a nice cold lager or a well chilled white wine.

Recipe Background

This is a firm favourite for a Saturday meal in our house, it's a nice easy going dinner, and much cheaper and healthier than a takeaway. You can make the chilli up in advance and warm through before eating, I think it tastes better this way but it could just be the anticipation.

Frikadeller

Submitted by Maureen Byrd, Blackthorn

4 tbsp breadcrumbs
1 cup water
1 lb pork mince
1 lb beef mince
1 large onion (finely chopped)

3 eggs
Salt and pepper
3 cups of full fat milk/single cream
Margarine/oil (to fry)

Cook on hob
Mixing bowl
Frying pan

Method

Put the breadcrumbs into a bowl and add the water and leave to soak for 20 minutes. Add the minced pork and beef and the chopped onion to the breadcrumbs and stir. Add in the eggs and the milk or cream and stir well until the mixture resembles a thick porridge. Season with salt and pepper. Take a tablespoon of the mixture and fry in a hot pan for 5-8 minutes on each side. Serve with home made spicy tomato sauce and a swirl of thick cream.

Recipe Background

This recipe is from friends in Denmark whose son and daughter stayed with us when taking part in a local scout jamboree. My sons have stayed in Denmark with them and are still in contact 40 years on.

Rogan Josh Lamb Curry

Submitted by Sue and Andy Sparkes, Blackthorn

3 tbsp vegetable oil
2 tsp fennel seeds
2 cinnamon sticks
6-8 green cardamom pods
6-8 cloves
3 fresh bay leaves
4 onions (peeled, halved and sliced)
1 kg leg or shoulder of lamb (boneless weight - cut into 2 cm cubes)
1 tbsp garlic paste (or 6 cloves bashed to a paste or grated)

1 tbsp ginger paste (or 2 inch piece bashed to a paste or grated)
2 tsp turmeric
Juice of ½ a lemon
1 tsp chilli powder
1 tsp salt
1 tsp ground cumin
2 tsp caster sugar
1 tsp ground coriander
1 tsp garam masala
3 tbsp tomato puree
Chopped fresh coriander (to serve)

Cook on hob
Large saucepan
Takes approximately 2 hours including preparation time

Serves 4

Method

Heat the oil in a large saucepan over a medium heat. Add the fennel, cinnamon, cardamom, cloves and bay leaves, and once they start to splutter add the onions and cook for about 15 minutes until lightly golden, stirring occasionally. Turn up the heat and add the meat and sear to seal it, and then cover with 1 cm boiling water. Bring up to a simmer, skimming off any impurities and simmer over a low heat uncovered for 40 minutes. Stir in the garlic and ginger pastes and simmer for another 20 minutes. Then stir in the remaining spices and the tomato puree and simmer for a further 20 minutes. Finally stir in the lemon juice, salt and sugar. Scatter over the garam masala, chopped coriander and serve with pilau rice.

Greek Lamb with Puntaletti

Submitted by Steve and Diane Procopiou, Blackthorn

500-750 g leg/shoulder of
lamb (cut into 4 cm cubes)
2 large onions (sliced)
2 tbsp fresh lemon juice
5-6 fresh oregano sprigs
2 tsp dried oregano
2 tsp cumin
2 tsp ground coriander

2 tbsp olive oil
2 tbsp tomato puree
900 ml boiling water
225 g puntaletti
Salt and pepper (seasoning)
Fresh oregano sprigs (to garnish)
Parmesan shavings (to serve)

Preheat oven to 180C
Large casserole dish

Serves 4

Method

Spread the lamb and onions in a casserole dish or small roasting tin. Sprinkle with the lemon juice, oregano, cumin, coriander and seasoning; mix well. Drizzle over the oil and roast, uncovered, for 1 hour (it will go black, but don't worry!). Dissolve the tomato puree in the boiling water and pour over the lamb. Return to the oven for 30 minutes. Sprinkle over the puntaletti, cover with a tight fitting lid or double thickness foil and cook for 20 minutes, by which time the puntaletti should be tender and most of the liquid absorbed (if necessary, add more

water and cook for a few minutes more, but don't let it dry out).
Taste and adjust seasoning. Serve hot from the dish garnished
with oregano sprigs and Parmesan shavings, accompanied by a
crisp green salad.

Top Tip

Puntaletti, or orzo, is tiny rice-shaped pasta, used in soup.
Naturally you can't get it in the local supermarkets, but
I've found it in the deli in the covered market in Oxford.
Alternatively you can buy it off the internet.

Greek Meatballs (Keftethakia)

Submitted by Tina Marinos, Friend of Blackthorn

400 g lamb mince (as lean as possible)
Parsley, mint salt and pepper (to taste)

200 g fresh breadcrumbs
1 egg (beaten)
1 clove of garlic (crushed)

Preheat oven to 180C
Large casserole dish

Serves 4

Method

Mix everything together and use the egg to bind the mixture. Form small balls about the size of a ping pong ball out of the mixture. Bake in the oven with a sprinkling of olive oil until brown (should take about 20 minutes). Can be eaten hot or cold.

Gammon in Claret

Submitted by Lawrence Beckett, Blackthorn

1 joint of unsmoked gammon
250-400 g suet (depending on
size of joint)
1 bottle of Claret wine

½ -1 tsp each (depending on
size of joint) of ground black
pepper, cloves and nutmeg

Preheat oven to 160C
Large roasting pan

Serves 4

Method

Choose a joint of unsmoked gammon. Soak the meat in water
for as long as possible before putting it into the oven. If it is
frozen defrost it thoroughly in water. Place the joint into the
roasting pan. Add the suet to half fill the pan. Add the Claret
wine. Don't cover the joint completely. Add spices. Cover and
place into the oven. Bake for at least 3 hours. The time and
temperature is an approximate guide only as they will depend
on your oven and the size of the joint. Turn the joint over
halfway through and check regularly. You may need to adjust
the temperature/time as pork should be cooked low and slow.
When finished any fat should fall away easily, the stock should

be nearly clear and the meat should pull apart with a spoon. Remove the joint, clear away any fat and leave it to cool. The meat will probably fall away in pieces rather than carve. Serve with roasted new potatoes (with onion, garlic and rosemary), vegetables and a poached apple.

Top Tip

When choosing a joint if it's on or off the bone it doesn't matter but a joint with a bone in will take less time to cook! Buy a piece of meat that is large enough, but make sure it fits easily into the casserole dish (with a lid). Make sure that the meat is about ready before preparing the vegetables. Poached apples take about 7-10 minutes in simmering water. Leave the skin on, slice them and serve with the meat.

Recipe Background

This is a traditional 16th century recipe that I have modernised. The original recipe was intended to preserve the gammon for 3-4 months but it tastes great straight out of the oven. This is a good alternative to the traditional Sunday roast. It was originally a pie recipe and the meat is cooked in fat, but it has a fantastic flavour. It takes less than 10 minutes to prepare but it needs to go in the oven about 4 hours before you want to sit down and eat.

Porc aux Tomates

Submitted by Ann Downham, Blackthorn

500 g-1 kg pork fillets
400 g tin chopped/whole
Italian plum tomatoes
12 small onions/shallots
(chopped onion will do but
not quite as nice)

1-2 garlic cloves (according to
taste - I use 2)
Sprigs fresh rosemary
Salt and pepper
Olive oil

Cook on hob
Casserole pan

1 fillet serves 2 people

Method

Trim any fat and fibre off the meat. Make small pockets with a sharp knife and insert garlic cloves. Turn the fillets in a mixture of salt and pepper. Heat 2-3 tbsp of olive oil in a casserole pan and brown the fillets all over. Turn the heat down; add tomatoes (with juice), onions/shallots, rosemary and more seasoning to taste. Cover the pan and cook gently for about 45 minutes to 1 hour. Test for tenderness, because size of fillets vary. Re-heats well.

Slow-Roasted Belly Pork with Apple Sauce

Submitted by Sue and Andy Sparkes, Blackthorn

5 lb piece of boned belly
pork
2 carrots (sliced lengthways
into quarters)
1 large onion (thickly sliced)
2 celery stalks (thickly sliced)
1 large leek (thickly sliced)
2 pt chicken stock

1 pt white wine
Sea salt and black pepper
6 dessert apples (peeled,
cored and sliced)
2 oz soft brown/Demerara
sugar
Large knob of butter
Juice of ½ a lemon

Preheat oven to 200C   Serves 4-6
Cook on the hob first, and then move to a preheated oven
Large saucepans
Large roasting tin

Method

Score the rind of the pork with a very sharp knife and rub some
sea salt into the scored fat. Place the pork in a large saucepan
and cover with cold water. Bring to the boil and simmer for 20
minutes. Drain and pat dry well using kitchen towel or a clean
tea towel. Place the carrots, onion celery and leek in a large
roasting tin and put pork on top, skin side up. Pour 3½ fl oz of

the chicken stock into the tin, place in the oven and roast for 10-20 minutes (on grill/roast function if you have it) until the fat has crisped up nicely. Keep checking so that it does not burn. Turn the oven down to160C and cook for a further 2 hours. Check every half hour or so and pour in a ladle of stock if required to keep the meat nice and moist.

For the apple sauce: Place the apple slices in a saucepan with a few tablespoons of water. Cover and cook gently until soft and pulpy. Beat the apples to make a smooth sauce, adding the sugar, butter and lemon juice to taste.

When ready to serve: Remove the pork from the roasting tin and cover with foil. Place the roasting tin on the hob. Heat gently scraping up all the caramelised vegetables and meat from the bottom of the tin. Add the white wine and simmer rapidly until reduced by half. Pour in the remaining stock and simmer for a further 5 minutes pressing the vegetables to a pulp to make gravy. Slice the pork and serve with the apple sauce, gravy and vegetables of your choosing.

Top Tip

When scoring the rind be careful not to cut right through the fat to the meat. Your butcher will be happy to do this for you - his knives will be much sharper than yours!

Breakfast Casserole

Submitted by Susan McKinney, Blackthorn

6 slices of bread (buttered on both sides)
1 lb of ground sausage (that has been cooked and drained)
One dozen eggs (beaten)

1½ cups Cheddar cheese (grated)
2 cups of milk
1 tsp salt
Pepper to taste

Preheat oven to 190C
Casserole dish

Serves 6

Method

Place the bread at the bottom of a casserole dish. Mix together all of the remaining ingredients. Pour over the bread. Bake for 45 minutes. Enjoy!!

Steak and Guinness Pie

Submitted by Michele Knox, Blackthorn

500-750g braising steak (cubed)
450 g Lincolnshire sausages cut into 4 pieces
1 bottle of Guinness

250 g mushrooms (sliced)
350 g ready rolled puff pastry
1 egg
Salt and pepper (to season)
Bisto powder

Preheat oven to 200C
Large saucepan
Deep pie dish

Serves 4-6

Method

Put the steak and Guinness into a pan and bring to the boil. Cover with a lid and simmer for approximately 1 hour. Add the sausages, mushrooms, pepper and salt if required. Continue to simmer until you can cut the steak with a dessert spoon (approximately another 45 minutes). Check the liquid level occasionally and add water if necessary. Add the Bisto powder to obtain the gravy consistency you like. Pour into a pie dish. Roll pastry out to approximately 3-4 cm larger than the pie dish and lay over the meat. Brush with the beaten egg and pierce a hole in the centre of the pastry. Decorate with pastry leaves. Bake until pastry is cooked and turns a golden brown (approximately 20-30 minutes).

Recipe Background

Adapted from
Granny's original
recipe where sausages
were added to
stretch out the beef.
Mushrooms were
added by me as I don't
like beef and wanted
to eat the same meal as
the rest of my family.

Honey Roasted Ham Hock

Submitted by Sue and Andy Sparkes, Blackthorn

2 small ham hocks
1 large onion (peeled and coarsely chopped)
1 large carrot (peeled and coarsely chopped)
4 cloves garlic (peeled)
1 sprig thyme

6 peppercorns
40 g English mustard
40 g French mustard
4 tbsp honey
100 g Demerara sugar
1 handful whole cloves
1 handful rosemary leaves

Cook on hob
Preheat oven to 190C
Large saucepan
Large roasting pan
Small bowl

Serves 4

Method

Rinse the ham hocks well under cold running water and put them into a large saucepan with the onion, carrot, garlic, thyme and peppercorns and pour in enough cold water to cover the meat. Bring to the boil then skim off any scum from the surface. Simmer, covered, for 3 hours until the hocks are very tender;

the bone should slide easily out of the meat. Leave the hocks to cool slightly in the liquid until you can handle them, then remove and peel off the skin, leaving the fat on. (Save the stock as this makes a great base for pea and ham soup). Score the fat on the hocks in a criss-cross pattern and put them in a large roasting pan.

In a small bowl, combine the two mustards, honey and Demerara sugar. Spread the mixture over the ham hocks and stud with the cloves and rosemary needles. Roast the hocks for 15-20 minutes until the glaze caramelises. Remove from the oven and leave to rest for about 5 minutes. Serve with creamy mash potato with Gruyere and spring onions.

Pork with Raisin Sauce

Submitted by Pat Tylor, Friend of Blackthorn

300 ml dry cider
50 g raisins
1 strip of lemon rind
4 pork chops

1 tbsp butter
1 tbsp arrowroot/cornflour
½ tsp dry mustard
Pinch of ground nutmeg

Cook on hob and under grill
Small heavy based saucepan
Small mixing bowl

Serves 4

Method

Place cider, raisins and lemon rind in a small heavy-based saucepan, bring to the boil and simmer for 10 minutes, then remove the rind. Meanwhile, prepare the chops and grill for 15-20 minutes, turning from time to time. Mix the arrowroot or cornflour and mustard to a paste with a little water. Stir in 1 tbsp of hot cider and then a little more before mixing the paste into the cider mixture. Bring the sauce to the boil, stirring constantly, and cook for one minute, and then add the nutmeg. When the chops are cooked, cut the butter into very small pieces and whisk into the sauce before pouring over the pork. This is a very tasty dish which can be served with sautéed potatoes and vegetables.

Cracked Potatoes

Submitted by Pat Tylor, Friend of Blackthorn

700 g new potatoes
Salt and ground black pepper
3 garlic cloves

Cook on hob
Preheat the oven to 190C
Saucepan
Frying pan
Roasting tin

Chopped onion
150 ml white wine
6 rosemary sprigs

Serves 6

Method

Cook potatoes in boiling salted water until just tender. Drain and
set aside. Heat the oil in a frying pan, add the onion and cook
for 4 minutes until soft. Add the crushed garlic and potatoes.
Using the back of a spoon, flatten each potato so it just cracks.
Add the wine and rosemary bring to the boil and reduce to
nothing. Place potatoes in a roasting tin, cover with foil and heat
in the oven for 35 minutes. Season and serve.

Recipe Background

A favourite of my wife's recipe collection, which went down a
treat and was always enjoyed by our guests.

Recipe Background

As students we were introduced to some of the first pizza restaurants. Back then options were limited to having 2 or 3 toppings on a pizza. We learnt to make our own as we wanted to try lots of toppings at the same time. We have been making our own pizzas ever since. You can put anything you want on a pizza and in any quantity but if you want a thin and crispy base don't overload it!

Perfect Pizza

Submitted by Andy and Anne Lee, Blackthorn

1 (500 g) packet of white bread mix (this will make 4-6 pizzas)
For each pizza: (quantities are approximate and can be changed according to taste)
2-3 tbsp of chopped tomatoes
½ tsp tomato puree
Pinch of paprika
Small red chilli (chopped finely - optional)
Small handful of sliced onions
Small handful of sliced peppers (red/green/yellow)
Small handful of sliced mushrooms

2-3 oz grated mozzarella cheese
2-3 oz grated Cheddar/ Double Gloucester cheese
6-8 thick slices of chorizo and zywiecka sausage (optional)
Small handful of seafood – prawns, mussels, etc (optional)
Few pieces of sun dried tomatoes (optional)
6-8 olives (optional)
Jalapeno peppers – quantity to your liking (optional)
½ tsp of oregano (optional)

Preheat oven to 220C
Baking sheet
Mixing bowl or bread making machine

Makes 1 large pizza

Method

Make bread dough as per instructions on the packet (by hand or in a bread making machine). When the dough has risen, divide into 4-6 pieces. Use 1 piece per pizza and freeze any that you don't need for future use. Grease and flour a metal baking sheet/tray. On a floured surface roll out dough to fit baking sheet, turning over at the edges to create a crust. Mix chopped tomatoes with tomato puree, paprika and red chilli. Spread tomato mixture onto pizza base and bake for 5-10 minutes, keeping an eye on it – the base needs to be crispy but not brown. Remove from the oven. Start to build up your pizza with sliced onions, peppers, jalapenos and mushrooms. Add the grated cheese. Finish with the sausage, seafood, sun dried tomatoes and olives. Sprinkle with oregano. Any of the toppings can be substituted with other items as desired. Place pizza back in the oven and bake for approximately 20 minutes until cheese is fully melted and bubbling. Check to make sure it doesn't burn. Slice and serve hot with a green salad.

Sun-Kissed Pork Chops

Submitted by Janet Heady, Friend of Blackthorn

4 pork chops
1½ level tbsp flour
Salt and pepper (to taste)
Orange slices/segments

½ cup orange juice
2-3 cups water
1 tsp soy sauce
Parsley

Cook on hob
Frying pan

Serves 4

Method

Trim pork chops and dust with ½ tbsp of flour. Fry chops in oil allowing 5 minutes each side. Lift out chops. Sprinkle remaining flour into pan and fry for 1 minute. Add orange juice, water, soy sauce and seasonings. Stir until gravy has thickened. Put chops back and cover and simmer gently for about 30 minutes or until chops are tender. Garnish with sprigs of parsley and slices/segments of orange.

Recipe Background

I've used this recipe for over a period of 50 years! It comes from a book of recipes gathered by members of the W.I. in Francis Town B.P. The title of the book is 'Recipes from Bechuanaland Protectorate' (now Botswana).

Gammon Brunch Potato Roast

Submitted by Maureen Byrd, Blackthorn

1 kg potatoes (Maris Piper)
6 tbsp oil
Salt and pepper
1 large onion (chopped)

1 each red, green and yellow
peppers
4 sausages
1 large gammon rasher

Preheat oven to 200C
Large roasting dish

Serves 4

Method

Peel potatoes and cut into even sized pieces. Deseed the peppers and cut into chunks. Cut each sausage into 4 pieces. Cut gammon rasher into strips. Heat 3 tbsp of the oil in roasting dish, add the potato pieces and coat in the oil. Roast for 30 minutes; turn the pieces over half way through. Mix together the remaining oil, peppers, onion and sausages and add to the potatoes. Season with salt and pepper and bake for a further 15 minutes. Add the gammon strips and cook for a further 15 minutes until the vegetables are cooked and the potatoes are crisp. Serve immediately.

Lentils and Rice

Submitted by Steve and Diane Procopiou, Blackthorn

1 onion
1 clove of garlic
3 rashers smoked streaky
bacon (optional)

Tomato puree
Stock
Green lentils
Rice

Cook on hob
Saucepan
Frying pan

Method

Rinse the lentils, put in a pan, cover with cold water and bring
to boil. Boil rapidly for 10 minutes, and then simmer until soft.
Chop the onion and crush the garlic; heat some oil and fry
gently until soft. Remove rind from the bacon, dice, and add
to the onion. Fry until the bacon is cooked, by which time the
lentils should also be ready. Add a good dollop of tomato puree
per person and fry for a few moments, and then add the rice,
stirring to coat. Season with pepper and a little salt. Add stock,
wine or water to cover the rice. Drain the lentils and stir into the
pan, making sure it's all covered in liquid. Cover and simmer
until the rice is cooked.

Add more liquid if it gets too dry, or boil it off if it's too wet when the rice is ready.

Top Tip

Use equal amounts of lentils and rice, about a heaped half cup per two people.

This is a good weekday supper recipe and can be varied according to what you have available. You can use chorizo, salami or any spicy sausage instead of the bacon. For a veggie version you can add ginger, ground cinnamon, cardamom, etc. for flavouring instead of the meat.

Max's Spanish Omelette

Submitted by Max Airey, Friend of Blackthorn

Olive oil
2-3 onions (chopped)
Several cloves of garlic
Peppers – red, green, yellow
or a combination (chopped)
Small cubes of potato
(essential) cooked for 5
minutes
Chopped tomatoes
(N.B. Not a tin, but fresh)

A few frozen peas
An appropriate number of
fresh eggs
Chopped and fried pieces
of smoked streaky bacon
(optional)
A smidgeon of mixed herbs
Freshly milled sea salt and
black pepper

Cook on hob
Finish under grill

Serves 2-10

Omelette pan or frying pan of a size appropriate to the number
of people you wish to serve

Method

Chop the onions as finely or as coarsely as you wish. Fry gently,
stirring occasionally, in good olive oil for 45-60 minutes on
lowest heat until it starts to caramelise. After 20 minutes chop or
crush the garlic and add this together with the chopped peppers
so that they are fully cooked through before the onions reach

their crescendo. Add the other ingredients, except the eggs, and make sure that everything is mixed well together. You may need to add more olive oil from time to time. When you are satisfied with your results, break 3-8 eggs into a bowl, depending on the number for whom you are catering, add the herbs, salt and pepper and break the yolks gently into the whites and mix them together for a short while (don't beat them). Pour this mixture into your omelette pan and make sure that everything is coated; using a spatula make sure that the egg mixture has penetrated to the bottom and commence to cook still on the same low heat. Depending on the size of the pan, it may be necessary to move the pan over the heat for 2 minutes or so at a time to ensure even cooking without burning. Heat the grill and transfer to finish off, rotating the pan to ensure an even browning of the top. Test with a knife to ensure that it is cooked throughout. Cut into slices and serve. It is not necessary to serve it with anything other than some crusty bread and butter, if you wish and some rough red wine (essential!).

Recipe Background

This recipe is a typical 'Poverty Dish' (as was paella, once upon a time) and is based on the fact that Spain was rich in onions, garlic, peppers, tomatoes and little else. You can add any protein-rich food to hand – bacon, ham, bits of chicken, sausage, prawns or whatever. Apart from the simplicity of the ingredients, it has the advantage, that, for a lot of the time, you can be doing other things, such as entertaining your guests. I consider that it is even better cold, with a salad, and it can be frozen too (though not if there is fish in it). So, Buen Apetito!

Penne with Pancetta and Goats' Cheese

Submitted by Sue and Andy Sparkes, Blackthorn

300 g dried penne (or other pasta shapes)
Smoked sea salt and black pepper
75 g butter
1 red chilli (trimmed, deseeded and finely chopped)
A few rosemary sprigs (leaves only, chopped)

250 g runner beans (trimmed and sliced on the diagonal)
100-150 g pancetta (diced)
Extra virgin olive oil (to drizzle)
150 g soft rindless goats' cheese log
50 g toasted pine nuts

Cook on hob
Large saucepan
2 frying pans

Serves 4

Method

Add the pasta to a large pan of boiling salted water and cook until al dente, between 8-12 minutes. Meanwhile, melt the butter in a large pan, add the chilli and rosemary and warm over a low heat for 1-2 minutes to let the flavours infuse. Turn up the heat, add the runner beans and cook for 3-4 minutes, stirring occasionally, until they are tender. In a separate pan crisp up the pancetta cubes. Drain the pasta and toss with a little olive oil, then mix with the beans.

Off the heat, crumble in the cheese, add the pancetta and toss to mix. Add a splash of boiling water if the sauce is too thick. Season with salt and pepper to taste. Scatter over pine nuts and serve.

Easy, peasy, lemon squeezy!! :)

Quicky Bacon Pudding

Submitted by Dulcie Hughes, Blackthorn

8 oz bacon rashers (chopped)
1 onion (chopped)
½ pt water (to boil)

5 oz self raising flour
2 oz butter

Cook on hob
Saucepan (with lid)
Mixing bowl

Serves 2

Method

Mix the flour and butter with a fork until crumbly. Add a little water to make a dumpling like dough. Put the bacon rashers and the chopped onion into a pan. Roll out and flatten the dough and cover the bacon rashers. Add the water, cover with a lid and simmer for 15 minutes.

Main Courses
- Vegetarian

Penny's Potato, Broccoli and Cheese Bake

Submitted by Penny Massingham, Friend of Blackthorn

12 oz potatoes (peeled and cut into cubes)
14 oz broccoli florets
1 onion (peeled and sliced)
3 cloves garlic (peeled and crushed)
7 oz cherry tomatoes (halved)/tin of cherry tomatoes (drained)
1-2 tbsp olive oil

4 oz of a good, tasty Cheddar cheese (grated)
7 oz frozen peas
3 large eggs
1 tsp dried chilli flakes/Very Lazy Chillies
7 oz crème fraiche
Handful of parsley (chopped)
Salt and black pepper

Preheat oven to 200C
Saucepan
Heavy frying pan
Large ovenproof dish
Mixing bowl

Serves 4

Method

Boil the cubed potatoes until tender, drain and set aside. Boil the broccoli for 2 minutes and drain. Oil a heavy frying pan and add the onions for 3 minutes over a medium to hot flame. Add the broccoli, tomatoes and peas and keep them moving for 2 minutes. Mix with the boiled potatoes and put into the ovenproof dish. Whisk up the eggs, chilli, crème fraiche and garlic until fairly smooth. Add the parsley, salt and ground black pepper. Pour over the other ingredients in the ovenproof dish and sprinkle with the cheese. Bake for 30 -35 minutes.

Top Tip

This makes a nice change for us non-veggies and is great if you are having a 'no meat' day. The chilli and garlic give it some oomph.

Carrot and Cashew Nut Roast

Submitted by Virginie Halphen, Blackthorn

45 g carrots (cooked and mashed)
225 g cashew nuts (ground)
1 medium onion (chopped)
2 cloves of garlic
1 tbsp olive oil
100 g wholewheat breadcrumbs

1 tbsp tahini
1½ tsp caraway seeds
1 tsp yeast extract
Juice of ½ a lemon
2½ fl oz stock from carrots
Salt and pepper

Preheat oven to 180C
Frying pan
900 g loaf tin

Serves 6

Method

Fry the onion and garlic in olive oil until soft and golden. Mix together with all the other ingredients and season to taste. Place the mixture in a greased loaf tin. Cover with foil and bake for 1 hour. Remove the foil and bake for another 10 minutes. Leave to stand in the baking tin for at least 10 minutes before turning out.

Phad Thai

Submitted by Sue and Andy Sparkes, Blackthorn

400 g Phad Thai flat noodles
2 handfuls of bean sprouts
2 red onions (halved and sliced)
4 eggs beaten (1 per person)
2 handfuls salted peanuts (lightly crushed)

4 spring onions (roughly chopped)
2 tbsp tamarind paste
Fish sauce
Light soy sauce
Sugar

Cook on hob
Wok or frying pan

Serves 6

Method

Soak the noodles in water for 30 minutes. Make some tamarind water by steeping 2 tbsp of tamarind paste in approximately 4 tbsp of warm water. Heat a couple of tbsp of vegetable oil in a wok or frying pan, add the sliced onions and beaten eggs. Stir until the onions have softened and the eggs have started to colour. Add the drained noodles and 2 tbsp of the tamarind water. Stir and warm through the noodles. Splash in 1 tbsp of fish sauce, 3-4 tbsp of light soy sauce and 2 heaped tbsp of sugar. Stir through and then add the bean sprouts and spring onions and serve.

Edam Bean Burgers

Submitted by Doreen Shirley, Friend of Blackthorn

100 g Edam cheese (very small cubes)
55 g pine nuts (toasted)
2 cans cannellini beans (drained and rinsed)
5 spring onions (chopped)
30 ml sundried tomato paste
75 g fresh breadcrumbs
1 egg (beaten)
Salt and pepper

Sunflower oil (frying)
4 ripe tomatoes (diced)
1 red pepper (deseeded and diced)
1 garlic clove (crushed)
3 tbsp flat leaf parsley (chopped)
1 tbsp olive oil
Juice of half a lemon

Cook on hob
Large non-stock frying pan
Large bowl

Method

Place the beans in a large bowl and mash well with potato masher or fork. Add the Edam, pine nuts, onion, tomato paste and a third of the breadcrumbs. Season and gently mix together until the ingredients are thoroughly combined. Shape the mixture into 8 burgers. Coat the outside of each burger first with the beaten egg, then with the remaining breadcrumbs. Cover and chill in the fridge for 20 minutes. Meanwhile, mix together the tomatoes, red pepper, garlic, parsley, olive oil and lemon juice, season well and set to one side. Heat sunflower oil in a large, non-stick frying pan and add the burgers. Fry for 3-4 minutes each side until golden and heated through. Drain on kitchen paper. Serve with favourite salad leaves and tomato relish in summer, or new potatoes and green beans in winter.

Potato Layer Bake

Submitted by Alison Durran, Friend of Blackthorn

1 kg potatoes (thinly sliced)
1 large onion (thinly sliced)
50 g butter
175 g mature Cheddar
cheese (grated)

300 ml milk
Salt and black pepper (to
season)

Preheat oven to 180C
Ovenproof dish

Serves 4

Method

Layer the potatoes, onion, butter and cheese in the dish, ending
with a layer of cheese. Season the milk and pour over the
potatoes. Bake for 1 hour and 30 minutes, until the potatoes
are cooked and the top has browned. Serve as an alternative to
dauphinoise potatoes with a Sunday roast.

Lightning Lentils

Submitted by Christine Neville, Friend of Blackthorn

4 oz red lentils
1 bay leaf
8 oz mushrooms
Soy sauce/tamari (to taste)

Cook on hob
2 saucepans

Method

Wash lentils and place in a pan with 2 cups of water and the
bay leaf. Bring to the boil and simmer for 15 minutes. Slice the
mushrooms and cook over a moderate heat. Reduce heat and
cover without adding water as the juice will 'sweat' out. After 4
minutes turn off the heat and stir the mushrooms into the lentils.
After 15-20 minutes, season with soy sauce/tamari. Serve with
pasta or jacket potato and salad or any other vegetable.

Top Tip

Cabbage can be used instead of mushrooms.

Creamy Gruyere Mash

Submitted by Sue and Andy Sparkes, Blackthorn

1 kg floury potatoes (such as King Edward, Maris Piper or Desiree)
100 g butter

100 ml double cream
4 spring onions (sliced)
100 g grated Gruyere

Cook on hob
Large saucepan with lid
Small saucepan

Serves 4

Method

Peel and cut the potatoes in to 4–6, depending on size. Put them in a large pan of cold water and bring up to the boil. Salt generously and cover with lid. Simmer until the potatoes are tender to the point of a knife. Drain and then return the potatoes to the pan and back on to the heat to briefly dry off further. Mash them with the butter using a metal potato masher, there should be no lumps. Warm through the cream in a separate pan and add to the mash. Stir through thoroughly. Fold in the grated cheese and sliced spring onions. Season to taste with salt and pepper and serve.

Dee's Red Cabbage

Submitted by Dee Richards, Blackthorn

1 medium sized red cabbage
(shredded)
4 cooking apples (cored and
chopped)
2 tbsp sugar

2 tbsp vinegar
2 tbsp water
1 tbsp butter
1 tsp all spice

Cook on hob
Large heavy bottomed non-stick saucepan

Method

Melt the butter in pan. Add all the other ingredients and mix well. Steam slowly. Can be served with a nut roast and all the trimmings. Cook for approximately 1 hour, longer if desired.

Jean Bannock's Fadge

Submitted by Edwin Bannock MBE, Blackthorn

1 lb cooked and mashed old
floury potatoes

4 oz plain flour
A pinch of salt (optional)

Cook on hob
Large mixing bowl
Large griddle or heavy based frying pan

Serves 4

Method

Combine the flour and potatoes in a large bowl until fully mixed
and forms a ball. Roll out the ball of mixture evenly until it is
approximately 5 mm in thickness. Cut into rounds to fit the
diameter of your pan (a large saucepan lid can be used for this).
Divide each round into 4 quarters. Dust the pan lightly with
a little plain flour and then heat on the hob. When the flour
begins to colour (pale beige) then the pan is ready for cooking.
Place the potato pancakes in the pan and cook until golden
brown. Turn over and repeat for the other side. Let these cool
and they can now be kept in the fridge for a week or frozen
to keep longer. To serve, fry gently in a hot lightly oiled pan
turning regularly to cook both sides. This only takes a couple of
minutes and enhances the golden colour.

This recipe can be made in larger batches for freezing. This is wonderful with a full English breakfast. Simple to make and very healthy, other than the bit of frying.

Recipe Background

This is another Ulster recipe handed down through my mum's family, making potatoes more interesting to eat.

Penny's Roasted Tomatoes

Submitted by Penny Massingham, Friend of Blackthorn

8 large beefsteak tomatoes	Salt and black pepper
Basil leaves	Olive oil and balsamic vinegar
3 cloves garlic (finely	(for dressing)
chopped)	Basil leaves (garnish)
Extra virgin olive oil	16 black olives (garnish)

Preheat oven to 200C
Shallow roasting dish

Serves 4

Method

Skin the tomatoes (make some cuts in the skin then pour boiling water over them and leave for a minute or so, drain and take off the skin). Cut each tomato in half and place cut side up in the roasting dish. Season with salt and black pepper. Sprinkle the chopped garlic on to the tomatoes then a few drops of olive oil on each plus a basil leaf (make sure the leaf is coated in oil too). Put into the oven for about 50 minutes, until the edges are slightly charred. Then take out and allow to cool.
You can do this part in advance if you like. We've tried this warm and cold, and cold just edges it.

When ready to serve, put 2 halves on each plate. Use fresh basil leaves and olives to garnish. Whisk up the olive oil and balsamic vinegar and drizzle over the tomatoes.

Top Tip

Goes well with a rustic Italian bread; well anything with a good crust really. Depending on what you are having as a main course, I find that a nice medium bodied wine like a Chianti or Merlot works well.

Mushroom Roulade

Submitted by Tamsin Addison, Blackthorn

For the Roulade:
Butter and Parmesan
shavings for coating
60 g cream cheese
150 ml single cream
4 free range eggs (separated)
200 g Gruyere/mature
Cheddar (grated)
3 tbsp fresh herbs (parsley,
thyme, marjoram)

Freshly grated Parmesan and
parsley (to garnish)
For the filling:
30 g butter
600 g mushrooms (sliced very
thinly)
2 garlic cloves (finely
chopped)
Salt and freshly ground black
pepper

Preheat oven to 200C
Swiss roll tin (greased and lined)
Large bowls
Saucepan

Serves 4

Method

To prepare the Swiss roll tin grease the paper lightly with melted
butter and dust with Parmesan cheese. Put the curd cheese
into a large bowl and add the cream slowly blending with each
addition to ensure mixture remains smooth. Beat the egg yolks
into mixture one by one. Stir in the grated cheese and the herbs.

In a separate bowl whisk the egg whites until they are stiff but not dry. Then fold the egg whites into the cheese mixture using a large metal spoon. Pour the egg and cheese mixture into the centre of the lined tin and then tilt tin to ensure that the mixture fills all the corners. Bake until risen and golden brown for 12-15 minutes. Once cooked place a piece of non-stick baking parchment on a clean flat surface and dust it with the remaining Parmesan. Turn the roulade out of the tin face down onto the dusted paper. Peel the parchment used to line the baking tin carefully from the back of the baked roulade. Leave to cool.

Melt the butter for the filling in a pan over a moderate heat. Add the sliced mushroom and the garlic, cook until the mushrooms are tender and the liquid has evaporated and season to taste. Cover the roulade with the cooled mushrooms and roll up (from short side) using the baking parchment to help lift and support the roulade as it is rolled. Ensure that the roulade seam is on the bottom to prevent it un-rolling. The roulade can be stored wrapped in the baking parchment for a day in the fridge. Alternatively wrap the roulade and parchment in silver foil and freeze. Serve warm or cold as required.

Recipe Background

This recipe was given to me by my mother-in-law and is now a classic for special occasions. We serve with red wine sauce as a vegetarian alternative for Christmas dinner.

Sticky Coconut Rice with Fresh Mango

Submitted by Sue and Andy Sparkes, Blackthorn

400 g of Thai glutinous rice
1 can of coconut milk
4 tbsp sugar

Pinch of salt
2 ripe mangos

Cook on hob
Steamer
Large saucepan

Serves 4

Method

Wash the rice twice and then cover in clean water and soak overnight. Drain the rice and put into a clean piece of muslin (or tea towel), twist cloth round and squeeze out as much excess water as you can. Place into a steamer and steam for 30-40 minutes. Bring the coconut milk to the boil add the sugar and a pinch of salt and stir. Put aside approximately 1 ramekin of coconut milk. Add the steamed rice to the remainder and stir through. Take off the heat. Peel and slice the mango and serve with the rice. Drizzle each serving with a spoonful or two of the reserved coconut milk.

Summer Vegetable Gratin

Submitted by Helen Prince, Friend of Blackthorn

2-3 courgettes/small aubergine (sliced ¼ inch)
2-3 yellow squash (sliced ¼ inch)
1 medium sweet onion (sliced ¼ inch)
1-2 tomatoes (sliced ¼ inch)

Grated Parmesan cheese
Salt and pepper
Olive oil
8 large fresh basil leaves (stacked, rolled, and cut into strips)
Breadcrumbs

Preheat oven to 180C
Earthenware dish to bake

Serves 4

Method

Coat a baking dish with olive oil spray. Begin layering courgettes to cover bottom, add salt and pepper, ¼ of the basil, handful of breadcrumbs, 1 tbsp of Parmesan cheese, and drizzle with olive oil. Then repeat with yellow squash, then with onion, and finish with tomato slices. Cover top of the tomato layer with a good covering of breadcrumbs and Parmesan.

Add remaining basil, drizzle with 2-3 tbsp of olive oil, and cover tightly with foil. Bake for 40 minutes. Uncover, raise heat to 190C and bake for an additional 15-20 minutes until breadcrumbs brown slightly and liquid in bottom of dish evaporates.

Champ (potatoes)

Submitted by Daphne Donnelly, Blackthorn

125 g spring onions
(chopped)
300 ml milk

6–8 potatoes
Salt and pepper
75 g butter

Cook on hob
Saucepan

Method

Boil the potatoes in salted water until just cooked, then mash.
Add the spring onions, together with the milk, which you have
heated separately. Season to taste with salt and pepper. Stir
in the butter or let it melt over the finished dish. Terrific with
something like lamb shanks or just on its own!

Recipe Background

My Mum's recipe from home in Ireland.

Butter Bean Loaf

Submitted by Doreen Shirley, Friend of Blackthorn

5 oz dried butterbeans
(soaked overnight and boiled
until soft)
1 medium onion (chopped
finely)
2 oz wholemeal breadcrumbs
2 oz grated vegetarian cheese

1 tbsp shoyu/soy sauce
1 tbsp tomato puree
½ tsp fresh sage/a pinch of
dried sage
¼ tsp ground black pepper
A little oil for frying

Preheat oven at 200C
Frying pan
Mixing bowl
Greased oven-proof dish

Serves 4

Method

Fry onion in oil until golden brown. Drain beans and mash
them well with a fork. Combine all ingredients together and mix
well. Press mixture together very well with hands and mould into
the shape of a Swiss roll. Place on a greased oven-proof dish
and cover lightly with greaseproof paper. Cook for 20 minutes.
Remove greaseproof paper and cook for a further 10 minutes
until the top is brown and crispy.

Top Tip

You can also use tinned butter beans. This is an excellent main dish which is very cheap and simple to prepare. It has a well balanced protein complement and is very versatile. It can be served hot with vegetables but it is equally delicious cold. It will keep for several days if kept in a fridge wrapped in foil. It can also be frozen.

Stuffed Pasta Shells

Submitted by Anthony Darvill, Friend of Blackthorn

500 g conchiglioni rigati pasta
250 g ricotta cheese
195 g Swiss cheese
175 g medium Cheddar
1 tin of chopped tomatoes
250 g broccoli

1 onion
½ tsp dried basil
½ tsp dried oregano
½ tsp dried mixed herbs
Salt and pepper (to taste)

Preheat oven to 200C
Large saucepan for pasta
Medium saucepan for broccoli
Mixing bowl
Large ovenproof dish

Serves 4

Method

Boil a pan of water and add a pinch of salt, then cook the pasta until al dente. Cut the broccoli into individual florets and cook in boiling water, until tender. Finely chop the onion and grate the cheese. Place the chopped onion and grated cheese into a large mixing bowl. Stir in the ricotta, add the herbs, salt and pepper and mix together. Once the broccoli is tender, drain and finely chop, then add to the mixture. Stir the mixture into a smooth paste, ready to fill the pasta shells. Drain pasta and allow to cool for a few minutes. Pour a can of chopped tomatoes into the large ovenproof dish and spread evenly. Stuff the shells with the mixture and gently close the shells. Place the shells into the dish, amongst the chopped tomatoes and bake on the middle shelf of the oven for 25 minutes. When ready arrange the shells on a plate and pour over any remaining tomatoes. Serve with a salad garnish.

Stovies

Submitted by Susan Henderson, Blackthorn

2 tbsp vegetable oil
1 lb 8 oz potatoes (sliced)

1 chopped onion
Salt and pepper

Cook on hob
Saucepan

Serves 4-6

Method

Heat the oil in a saucepan and cook the onion until soft and just turning brown. Add the sliced potato and mix thoroughly with onions. Pour enough water over to nearly cover potato mixture. Season well. Cover pan, bring to boil then turn down low and cook for about 30 minutes until potatoes are soft.

Mushroom Feast

Submitted by Alex Grell, Blackthorn

4 cups mushrooms (sliced)
½ cup onions (finely
chopped)
½ cup parsley (coarsely
chopped)
1 garlic clove (finely
chopped)
2 tbsp olive oil

1 tsp thyme
1 tsp fresh rosemary (finely
chopped)
¼ cup dry white wine
½ cup crème fraiche
½ cup double cream
Salt and pepper (to season)

Cook on hob
Large frying pan

Serves 4

Method

Put the butter and the olive oil in a frying pan and melt over
medium heat, add the onions and slowly cook until translucent
Add the garlic and rosemary and cook for 3-4 minutes, then turn
up the heat and add the wine. Let the alcohol evaporate before
turning the heat down to medium and add the mushrooms
and thyme. Slowly cook, stirring occasionally for a few minutes
until the mushrooms have soaked up the juices in the pan and
begin to release their water. Add the crème fraiche and ¾ of
the parsley, mix well. After another 1-2 minutes, add the cream

and bring to a gentle simmer. Taste, season with salt and pepper and let simmer until the sauce is reduced to a thick, creamy consistency. Serve immediately, sprinkle generously with the remaining parsley.

Recipe Background

I grew up in Germany and will always remember Sunday walks with my parents, looking for mushrooms in fields and forests on the way. We would always carry little wicker baskets with us to put the mushrooms in. Once back home, my mother or grandmother would go straight to the kitchen and prepare a wonderful dinner with the day's takings of wild mushrooms. There are many fantastic recipes for dishes with mushrooms around, but this is our favourite because it focuses on the flavour of the mushrooms themselves, the rest of the ingredients merely enhance and support these flavours. Button mushrooms are sufficient for this dish but things are changing in the English supermarket landscape and more and more mushroom types are becoming available, so be brave and try to add some other varieties. Guten Appettit!

.

Sweet Things
- Desserts

Amarula Affogato

Submitted by Ben Lee, Blackthorn

2 scoops of vanilla ice cream
1-2 shots of Amarula liqueur
1 shot of freshly brewed
espresso coffee
Strawberry (to decorate)

Serving glass (or cup)   Serves 1

Method

Make the coffee and leave to cool slightly. Place the ice cream
into the glass/cup. Pour the Amarula liqueur over the ice cream.
Pour the coffee over the ice cream. Partially slice the strawberry
and place it on the rim of the glass as a garnish.

Recipe Background

I picked up the recipe for Affogato (Italian for 'drowned') when
working as a waiter in a local restaurant. I always recommended
it because it is delicious and easy to make! This recipe uses
Amarula which is an African cream liqueur made from the fruit
of the Marula tree. This fruit is a favourite of elephants who will
shake the tree to access it.

Celebration Lemon Roulade

Submitted by Ruth Harris, CAFE, Friend of Blackthorn

2 oz butter (softened)
4 oz caster sugar
2 eggs
4 oz self raising flour (sifted)
Grated rind and zest of
1 lemon (reserve juice for
lemon curd)
1 tbsp hot water
2 eggs
3 oz caster sugar

Zest of 2 lemons
2 oz butter (softened)
1 tub of mascarpone (well
chilled)
1 tub of fromage frais (8% fat
content, well chilled)
1 dsp caster sugar
2 oz icing sugar (sifted)
Zest and juice of 1 lemon

Preheat oven to 200C
Heatproof bowl
Saucepan
Mixing bowl
Shallow baking tray (grease and line with baking parchment, and
grease that with melted butter)

Method

To make the lemon curd: Sit a heatproof bowl over a pan of
barely boiling water, but don't let the bowl touch the water. Put
2 eggs, 3 oz sugar, zest of 2 lemons, and the juice of 1 lemon in a

bowl and whisk together. Add butter in small pieces, and give a good whisk for about 10 minutes, until curd is smooth. Remove bowl from water and allow to cool. When cool, press cling film over surface and chill in fridge.

To make the sponge: put 2 oz of butter and 4 oz of sugar in bowl and cream together. Add 2 eggs and beat. Sift in the flour and stir well. Add water and whisk. Put mixture in prepared tin, and bake on centre shelf for 8-10 minutes. When ready it should be springy to touch. Remove from oven and allow to cool for 5 minutes. Turn out onto piece of parchment paper dusted with icing sugar. Cover sponge with damp tea towel for 5 minutes only. Spread with ¾ lemon curd. Whisk mascarpone, fromage frais and dessert spoon of sugar together and spread ¾ of that over lemon curd. Carefully roll up the roulade (loosely). Place lemon zest in saucer with lemon juice. In a bowl mix icing sugar with 1½ dessert spoons of lemon juice to make a thin glaze. Drizzle this over cake, drain lemon zest and scatter over icing. Mix the remaining lemon curd and mascarpone cream together and serve separately.

Crème Velour

Submitted by Suzanne O'Driscoll, Blackthorn

6 oz cream cheese
1½ oz caster sugar
2 large eggs
½ pt of double cream

2½ oz good dessert chocolate
1 oz crushed walnuts
2 tbsp brandy/sherry

Mixing bowl

Method

Beat the sugar into the cream cheese until it is smooth. Separate the eggs and beat in egg yolks one at a time, until the mixture is creamy. Whip the cream until fairly stiff and continuing to blend in the cream cheese mixture. Break chocolate into small pieces and melt with a tbsp of water over low heat or in microwave. Stir melted chocolate into cheese mixture with crushed walnuts and sherry or brandy. Whip egg whites until they are very stiff and fold them into the mixture. Pour into individual or one glass bowl and chill in fridge for 2-3 hours. Decorate with chopped walnuts and/or flaked chocolate.

Note: uncooked eggs.

Lemon Cheesecake

Submitted by Karen Jobling, Blackthorn

½ lb digestive biscuits
(crushed)
¼ lb butter/margarine
½ lb cream cheese
½ lb caster sugar

1 lemon jelly
2 lemons (juice and zest)
Large tin of condensed milk
(chilled in the fridge)

8-10 inch flan tin with removable base
Mixing bowls

Method

Melt butter and add to crushed biscuits. Put biscuit mixture into the flan tin and press down. Dissolve jelly in ¼ pint of boiling water. Add juice and zest of the lemons. Beat cheese and sugar together. Whip condensed milk as much as possible, and gradually add to the cheese mixture. Slowly add the jelly and lemons and then beat well together. Pour onto the biscuit base. Chill for 2 hours in the fridge.

Penny's Berry Terrine

Submitted by Penny Massingham, Friend of Blackthorn

1 lb of mixed berries
(blueberries, redcurrants
and raspberries or whatever
berries you can source)

2 sachets of strawberry/
raspberry jelly (sugar free,
optional)
2 tbsp powdered gelatine

Medium sized loaf tin

Serves 4

Method

Put the berries in loaf tin and chill (the loaf tin, not you!).
Make up the jelly according to the instructions and sprinkle
the gelatine over it, stir well and allow to cool. Once cooled
pour it into the loaf tin, over the chilled fruit. Put it in the fridge
(overnight is best) until set. When ready to serve dip the tin
into hot water and turn out onto a serving plate. Slice and serve.
Cream works well with this, or crème fraiche if you have the will
power.

Lemon and Orange Mousse

Submitted by Cynthia O'Driscoll, Blackthorn

Finely grated rind of
2 oranges, 1 lemon and their
juice
Extra orange and lemon juice
might be needed from either
more fruit or a carton

4 eggs (separated)
4 oz caster sugar
1 tsp of gelatine powder
½ pt of whipping cream

Heatproof bowls
Saucepan
Mixing bowls

Serves 6-8

Method

Take juice from the oranges and lemon to make ½ pt (if low
top up with extra juice). Beat egg yolks and sugar (in heat proof
bowl) over a pan of simmering water, until mixture thickens
(approximately 10-15 minutes). Pour 4 tbsp from the fruit juice
into separate heat proof bowl and sprinkle on the gelatine. Soak
for 5 minutes and then stand heat proof bowl in hot water, until
gelatine melts. Stir gelatine into egg mixture, and then stir in
juices and grated rinds. Whip cream until it holds shape. Whisk
egg whites until stiff peaks. Fold cream into orange mixture.
Fold egg whites into mixture. Pour mousse mixture into serving

glass bowl and put in fridge for 4 hours. Decorate top with dry cooled strips of orange and lemon rind, after blanching in boiling water for 3 minutes.

Recipe Background

A really refreshing dessert, quite a lot of preparation but this mousse has been a great favourite and a recipe which is often passed onto friends.

Rice Pudding

Submitted by Alison Durran, Blackthorn

50 g pudding rice
25 g butter
50 g sugar
500 ml full fat milk
50 ml boiling water
1 tsp nutmeg (optional)

Preheat oven to 160C
1 ltr ovenproof dish

Method

Place rice and sugar into ovenproof dish and pour on the water and dissolve the sugar. Pour milk over the rice and stir. Put the butter on the top in small pieces and sprinkle over the nutmeg. Place on the middle shelf of the oven and bake for 2 hours.

Sandie's Summer Pudding

Submitted by Sandie Stevenson, Blackthorn

1 pack sponge fingers/small
homemade sponge
1 mango (skinned, stoned
and sliced)
1 nectarine (skinned, stoned
and sliced)
1 peach (skinned, stoned and
sliced)

Strawberries
Redcurrants
Raspberries
Blackberries
3 g sugar
Honey
Cointreau
Cream/ice cream

Large deep dish
Saucepan

Method

Lay sponge fingers in dish and layer on the mango, nectarine
and peach slices. Put the berries and redcurrants (leave some
aside for decoration) into a pan and boil lightly with sugar and
honey. Pour the cooked fruit over the sponge and fresh fruit
and allow the sponge to soak up all the juices. Chill overnight.
Remove from the fridge pour over a shot of Cointreau and
decorate with the remainder of the fruit. Serve with single cream
or vanilla ice cream, or both!

Syrup Sponge Pudding

Submitted by Doreen Teckoe, Blackthorn

100 g softened butter
100 g light brown sugar
2 eggs (beaten)
100 g self raising flour

1.25–2.5 ml vanilla flavouring
15 ml milk
30 ml syrup

Cook in microwave
Mixing bowl
Large ovenproof pudding basin

Serves 4

Method

Grease the pudding basin. Beat together the butter and sugar until light and fluffy. Add a little of the beaten egg and 1 tbsp of the flour and beat again. Add in the remaining egg and fold in the rest of the flour. Blend the vanilla essence and milk together and stir into the mixture to form a heavy batter. Put the syrup into the base of the pudding basin and spoon the batter mix on top. Cover the basin loosely with cling film, pressing it close in at the sides of the basin but pulling it high above the centre of the pudding so that it is very loose and wrinkly. Microwave on high for 3 minutes (the pudding should be dry on top and shrink away from the sides of the basin). Leave to stand for 5 minutes and turn out onto a warm dish. Serve with ice cream or custard.

Sticky Toffee Pudding

Submitted by Ruth and Tim Harvey, Blackthorn

6 oz stoned dates (chopped
in packet are the easiest)
6 oz granulated sugar
½ pt boiling water
2 oz butter
8 oz self raising flour
1 large egg

1 tsp vanilla essence
½ tsp bicarbonate of soda
5 oz soft brown sugar
3 oz butter
4 tbsp double cream

Preheat oven to 180C
Mixing bowl
Large baking tin (well buttered)
Heavy bottomed non-stick saucepan

Serves 4

Method

Soak dates in boiling water for at least 20 minutes. In a separate
bowl cream butter and sugar together, until light and fluffy, then
beat in egg. Sift in flour and stir. Add vanilla to the drained dates
and then add bicarbonate of soda and stir well. Tip everything in
together and mix well until you have a battery texture. Put into
the buttered tin and bake for 35 minutes. While it's cooking put

the brown sugar, butter and double cream into saucepan and melt together. When pudding is cooked turn it onto a plate, or cut to individual portions and pour over sauce!

Top Tip

If you want to re-heat the pudding, a turned off oven after a roast will be hot enough.

Recipe Background

This recipe was given to me by our good friend Damon Hill; all racing drivers (let's face it, all men) love their puddings!

Drambuie Custard

Submitted by Bruce Knox, Blackthorn

1 pt milk
2 fl oz single cream
1 vanilla pod
6-7 free range bantam egg
yolks

1 oz caster sugar
2 level tsp cornflour
4 generous tbsp of Drambuie

Mixing bowl
Cup
Heavy bottomed non-stick saucepan

Method

Mix the cornflour and 2 tbsp of milk to a smooth paste in a cup.
Put the remaining milk, cream and vanilla pod into a pan and
bring to simmering point slowly over a low heat. Don't let it boil!
Remove the vanilla pod then wash and dry it. Put it in a sealed
container with the caster sugar and shake for 5-10 minutes. Beat
the yolks, sugar and cornflour paste together in a bowl until
well blended. Pour the hot milk and cream on to the eggs and
sugar, whisking all the time with a whisk. Return to the pan,
(add vanilla extract if using) and over a low heat gently stir with
a wooden spoon until thickened. Add the Drambuie just as it
starts to thicken. Pour the custard into a jug and serve at once.

Ginger Shortbread Fruit Pie

Submitted by Michele Knox, Blackthorn

350 g plain flour
225 g butter
50-75 g caster sugar
2-3 globes of stem ginger
(drained and finely chopped)

450 g blueberries and
blackberries from the hedges
of Blackthorn
icing sugar

Preheat oven to 180C
Mixing bowl
Rolling pin and board
Individual pie dishes
Baking beans

Method

Sieve the flour into the mixing bowl and rub in the butter until
it resembles breadcrumbs. Stir in the sugar and the ginger.
Knead together until a ball is formed. Roll out approx. 5 mm
thick. Grease and line the pie dishes with the shortbread.
The shortbread will break so just patch it or pinch it together
as required. Prick the base with a fork and add the baking
beans. Bake for 10-15 mins. until lightly golden. Remove and
leave to cool. Stack high with berries and sprinkle with icing
sugar and serve with Drambuie custard.

Bread Pudding

Submitted by Doris Higgins, Blackthorn

½ a loaf of bread
4 oz flour
8 oz sultanas
4 oz sugar

4 oz margarine (melted)
Water (to soak bread)
2 eggs

Preheat oven to 150C
Mixing bowl
Cake tin (greased and lined)

Serves 4

Method

Soak bread in water for 5-10 minutes (tip any excess water away).
Mix all the ingredients one by one into the soaked bread. Beat
well. Turn mixture into the tin and bake for 1 hour 15 minutes.
Serve warm with cream or eat cold. Both are delicious!

Recipe Background

This was my grannie's recipe, a firm family favourite; it was
passed on to me by my mother and I have passed it on to my
children.

Ginger Lemon Pudding

Submitted by Dorothy Boyd, Friend of Blackthorn

250 g ginger biscuits
50 g butter (melted)
1 tin of condensed milk

250 ml double cream
Zest of 3 lemons
150 ml lemon juice

Mixing bowl
20 cm baking tin

Method

Crush the biscuits with a rolling pin and put into a bowl. Add melted butter and press mixture into the tin to form a biscuit base. Mix the condensed milk, cream, lemon juice and zest together and stir until the mixture thickens. Pour over the biscuit base and leave in the fridge to set overnight.

Hawaiian Surprise

Submitted by Jean Cross, Blackthorn

For crust:
12 digestive biscuits
3 oz of butter
½ cup of sugar
For filling:
3 oz of butter

1½ cups of icing sugar
½ cup of nuts
1 cup/tin of crushed pineapple
Whipped cream
2 eggs (well beaten)

Preheat oven to 190C
Mixing bowl
Baking sheet/cake tin

Serves 4

Method

With rolling pin crush biscuits. Stir in sugar and butter then bake for 5 minutes. For the filling: Cream the butter and icing sugar together. Add in the beaten eggs and mix . Then spread over the crust. Finally add crushed pineapple and cover with cream as well as nuts. Note: uncooked eggs.

Recipe Background

This recipe was given to me by my step mother-in-law, Wendy Cross when Michael and I were just married in 1979.

Mike's Barbequed Bananas

Submitted by Mike and Gail Groom, Blackthorn

10 Bananas
100 g brown sugar
150 ml Jamaican rum

Cook on barbecue   Serves 10

Method

Use one large banana for each person. With the banana lying
flat, cut out an elliptical piece of skin from the top (so it looks
like a curved canoe!) With a small knife, score the exposed flesh
in a diamond pattern. Sprinkle 10 g of soft brown sugar onto the
exposed flesh of each banana. Carefully pour 15 ml of Jamaican
rum on top of the sugar, so all the sugar is saturated on each
banana. Place the bananas onto the barbeque rack (best when
the coal fire has died down a little). Cook until the whole of
the skin has turned brown and the flesh is soft. Serve and enjoy
(perhaps with ice cream).

Top Tip

You can add a little rum while cooking, but watch out for
ignition as you may have your eyebrows removed! We feel
each banana being served with a scoop of vanilla ice cream is
delicious!

Max's Hot Summer Fruit Pudding

Submitted by Max Airey, Friend of Blackthorn

Some soft bananas
Freshly squeezed orange
juice
Sliced green and red apples
(with skin on)

Any available summer soft
fruits (nectarines, peaches,
apricots etc)
Cointreau

Cook on hob
Large frying pan
Takes about 40 minutes

Serves as many as you wish

Method

Place the sliced bananas in the frying pan with the orange juice
and simmer until you have a mush. Add the prepared apples
and simmer until they are becoming soft. Add the softer fruit
and continue to simmer until all are soft. You may need to add
extra orange juice. When you think it is ready, put in a large slug
of Cointreau and set fire to it. When the flames die down, it is
ready.

It can be prepared before the guests arrive and kept warm (another slug of liquor can be added if this is the case) alternatively serve fridge-cold; it is certainly good eaten cold.

Top Tip

The art lies in having the mixture multi-coloured and flavoured and in having the fruits soft at the same time (for example, apricots tend to be harder than nectarines, which are themselves harder than peaches).

Recipe Background

This was invented by a friend who tried always to have alcohol in his food, as well as in a glass by the side of it. As the alcohol burns off, you need not feel guilty about its inclusion in food!

Apricot and Apple Crumble

Submitted by Doreen Shirley, Friend of Blackthorn

4 oz wholemeal flour
4 oz dried apricots (chopped)
2 oz rolled oats
1 lb cooking apples (sliced)
2 oz margarine
2 oz dates (chopped)

1 tbsp sesame seeds
1 tbsp lemon juice
2 oz soft brown sugar
½ pt water
½ tsp ground cinnamon

Preheat oven to 200C
Mixing bowl
Pressure cooker or saucepan
Casserole dish

Method

Combine the flour and oats and rub in the margarine to make a crumble. Add the sesame seeds, sugar and cinnamon and mix well. Put the apricots, apples, dates, lemon juice and water into a pressure cooker or ordinary saucepan. Bring up to pressure and cook for 5 minutes, or 20 minutes in an ordinary saucepan. Transfer the mixture to a casserole dish, cover with the prepared crumble and bake for 25 minutes.

Torte Del Amandes

Submitted by Jenny Thompson, Blackthorn

4 eggs	Grated zest of an orange/
½ lb caster sugar	lemon
250 g ground almonds	A few drops almond essence

Preheat oven to 170C   Serves 8-10

Mixing bowl

8 or 9 inch loose bottomed tin (greased and lined)

Method

Whisk eggs to frothiness. Gradually stir and whisk in sugar. Fold in almonds, zest and essence. Pour into prepared tin and bake for roughly 40 minutes depending on oven and until a nice light brown colour on top, with a slight crust to it. It won't rise so do expect a flat cake! Allow to cool then take out of tin. To serve decorate with a sprinkling of icing sugar and perhaps raspberries plopped on at the last minute. This is a beautifully moist cake and could be served as a cake or dessert with crème fraiche or perhaps crème anglaise, or whatever else may take your fancy!

Easy Peasy Banoffee Pie

Submitted by Rachel Lamont, Blackthorn

1 pack of biscuits (digestive
or rich tea)
1 large knob of butter
4 bananas

1 can of Carnation caramel
1 pot of whipping cream/can
of squirty cream

Saucepan
Large serving dish
Electric whisk
Piping bag

Method

Crush the biscuits until like fine breadcrumbs. Put the knob of
butter into the saucepan and melt. Mix the biscuit crumbs and
melted butter together to form a smooth paste and spoon evenly
into the bottom of the serving dish. Chill until the base is set.
Chop the bananas into even slices and arrange over the biscuit
base. Open the can of caramel and spread neatly over the top of
the bananas. Whisk the cream until light and fluffy and pipe on
to the top. Serve chilled with more cream or ice cream.

Top Tip

You can buy condensed milk and make your own caramel but buying the ready made stuff is so much easier! If you're feeling really lazy just use the squirty cream on top.

Recipe Background

When I first made this dish it went horribly wrong, as I tried to make my own caramel using condensed milk. After boiling the tin for over 2 hours I opened it expecting to see gooey caramel and was sorely disappointed with the warm condensed milk. I have since perfected the recipe by using the ready made stuff! A firm favourite of Gareth's.

Sally's Lemon Cheesecake

Submitted by Jenny Thompson, Blackthorn

200 g ginger nut biscuits
200 g digestive biscuits
110 g salted butter
1 tbsp golden syrup
500 g full fat mascarpone cheese

9 inch loose bottomed tin
Heavy bottomed saucepan
Mixing bowl

1 350 g tin of condensed milk
Juice of 4-6 lemons (to taste - which can be tricky as the taste melds and develops over time)
Zest of 2-3 lemons

Serves 10+

Method

For the base: smash up biscuits. Melt butter and golden syrup gently and mix into biscuits. Once all coated press reasonably firmly into tin. Allow to cool before putting into fridge for 1-2 hours until set.

For the filling: whisk together mascarpone, condensed milk and zest. Gradually whisk in lemon juice to taste which can be rather tart and may be slightly off putting, but I promise the taste really does develop over time. Pour over base and chill in fridge, preferably for a day.

Top Tip

When chilling, ensure the tin is on a plate as this delicious
syrupy, gingery goo seeps out from the base, which is the chef's
treat! This pudding really benefits from being made a day in
advance of the eating! To serve decorate however you wish,
for whatever time of year it may be for. I've given this recipe to
the Henderson's son Toby and his wife Jo and they've taken to
serving it with holly at Christmas, chocolate eggs at Easter and
with fruit for summer parties! A very versatile pud that also goes
a long way - and no baking!

Recipe Background

This comes from our good friend Sally who lives nearby in
Marsh Gibbon and from whom years ago I said please could I
have the recipe. Sally and her husband Peter have come along to
some of our Blackthorn events and then cycled carefully home!

Passion Fruit and Mango Roulade

Submitted by Daphne Donnelly, Blackthorn

3 egg whites
175 g caster sugar
1 tsp cornflour
1 tsp vinegar

Icing sugar (to dust)
200 g double whipped cream
1 ripe mango (finely chopped)
4 passion fruits (insides only)

Mixing bowl
Swiss roll tin (greased and lined)
Preheat the oven to 150C (fan 130C)

Serves 6

Method

Beat the egg whites with a whisk until they are fluffy. Continue to whisk slowly while adding the caster sugar (a little at a time). Fold in the cornflour and vinegar. Gently spoon the mixture into the tin and level the surface carefully. Make sure you don't push out the air. Bake for 30 minutes until the meringue surface is just firm. Remove from the oven and cover with damp greaseproof paper for 10 minutes. Dust another sheet of greaseproof paper with some icing sugar and then turn the meringue out on to the sugar coated paper. Peel off the lining paper, spread the cream over the meringue and spoon on the finely chopped fruit. Using the paper, roll up the roulade from one short end. Keep the join underneath. Sift a little icing sugar on top.

Australian Pavlova

Submitted by The Whites, in memory of Joyce White, Blackthorn

2 egg whites
1½ cups sugar (granulated or caster)
1 tsp vinegar

4 tsp cornflour
½ tsp vanilla
4 tbsp boiling water
Fruit and cream (to serve)

Preheat oven to 150C
Mixing bowl

Method

Put all ingredients together in a bowl and beat for 15 minutes. Place mixture on to a well greased, medium sized dinner plate and cook for 10 minutes. Reduce heat to as low as possible and cook for a further 45 minutes. When cold, decorate with fresh or tinned fruit and cream.

Vacherin Maison

Submitted by Virginie Halphen, Blackthorn

4 eggs
3 tbsp of vanilla sugar
20 cl of double cream
9 tbsp of icing sugar
100 g of meringues

250 g of raspberries
2 tbsp of Grand Marnier or
Cointreau
2 tbsp of icing sugar
2 tsp of lemon juice

Set in freezer
Large bowls
Container for freezing
Blender

Method

In a large bowl, beat egg yolks with vanilla sugar. Add the double
cream. In a separate bowl beat egg whites until very stiff and add
icing sugar. Add to the preparation. Pour half of this mixture
into a container, cover with half of the meringues, pour over the
second half of the mixture and add the remaining meringues.
Put in the freezer for 4-5 hours. In the meantime, make the
raspberry puree. Blend the raspberries in a mixer without
forgetting to put some aside for decoration. Add the Grand
Marnier or Cointreau, the lemon juice, the icing sugar and
stir well in order to obtain a smooth puree, keep aside. Take

container out of freezer and remove dessert. Decorate with the raspberry puree. Add some fresh raspberries on top.

Recipe Background

This is a recipe my sister Valérie sent me from France. She told me it was a great recipe because it was easy to make, almost impossible to fail, and made a good looking pudding which tastes delicious.

What more do we want!

Lemon Meringue Roulade

Submitted by June Foreman, Tailor Made Catering Solutions

6 egg whites
13 oz caster sugar
1 tsp cornflour
1 tsp white wine vinegar

A little vanilla essence
Lemon curd
Whipped cream

Preheat oven to 120C
Mixing bowl
Large baking tray

Serves 10–15

Method

First prepare your baking tray. For this quantity, I use the pan
from my grill which measures 12x15 inches and is about 1 inch
deep, and line it with baking parchment. Whisk egg whites
until fairly stiff, very gradually add sugar a little at a time, then
cornflour, vinegar and vanilla. Spread into prepared tin and
smooth with a palette knife. Cook for 50-60 minutes. Take out
of oven and place the tray on a cooling rack then cover it all
with foil and leave for at least one hour and up to 24 hours. To
complete put cling film (you may need to put two pieces side by
side if the cling film is not wide enough) onto work surface, sieve
icing sugar over it and up end the roulade onto this. Remove

baking parchment carefully. Spread the meringue with lemon curd (I make my own it is much tangier than bought) then with whipped cream. Use the cling film to help roll up the roulade. Place on a serving dish pipe rosettes of cream on top and put a quarter of a strawberry on each rosette with a sprig of mint.

Top Tip

This freezes beautifully and takes little time to thaw; decorate after thawing.

Rhubarb and Strawberry Compote

From John and Naomi Karslake, Blackthorn

1 kg rhubarb
500 g sugar
500 g strawberries
2 oranges

1 tub crème fraiche
Soft brown sugar (to decorate)

Cook on hob
Large saucepan

Method

Chop rhubarb into 1 inch pieces and stew gently with the juice from the oranges and the sugar for 5 minutes, until just soft. Cut the strawberries in half and add to the stewed rhubarb. Set aside to cool. Serve with crème fraiche and soft brown sugar.

Sweet Things
- Cakes

Monty's Pancakes

Submitted by Monty Lamont, Blackthorn

4 oz plain flour
1 egg
Pinch of salt

½ pt liquid (made up of half
milk and half water)
Oil (for cooking)

Cook on the hob
Frying pan

Method

Mix together the dry ingredients and make a well in the centre.
Beat the egg with a little of the liquid and drop into the dry
ingredients. Stir until combined. Gradually add the rest of the
liquid, until a single cream consistency is achieved. Whisk the
mixture thoroughly and chill for 20 minutes. When ready to
cook give the mix a final whisk. Heat a little oil in the pan and
using a ladle add some of the batter mix. Spread the mixture
evenly over the bottom of the pan, cook for about 1 minute,
then the pancake will need flipping over (you can do this with
a spatula, but its much more fun to flip it using the pan). Cook
the other side for 1 minute, or until golden brown. Serve
immediately with whatever takes your fancy (my favourites are
maple syrup or sugar and freshly squeezed lemon juice).

Top Tip

Make sure the pan is really hot and don't use too much oil. If you decide to toss the pancake instead of using a spatula, make sure you have a mop handy!!

Recipe Background

You've no doubt seen me at village social events stood in front of the portable gas stove knocking out hundreds of these; who doesn't love pancakes? The art in pancake making is the mix of water and milk and ensuring that the mixture is the right consistency: too thin and they don't work too thick and you end up with Yorkshire puddings - a little known family secret!

Barm Brack

Submitted by Hilary Wright, Blackthorn

¾ pt of cold tea
7 oz soft brown sugar
12 oz mixed dried fruit

10 oz self raising flour
1 egg

Preheat oven to 180C
Bowl
8 inch round or 2 lb loaf tin (greased well)

Method

Put tea, sugar and dried fruit in a bowl, cover and leave to soak overnight (tea that has been left over during the day can be saved and used). Mix the soaked fruit and sugar plus the liquid into the flour. Add the beaten egg to make a smooth mixture. Turn into the tin and bake in a moderate oven for about 1 hour 45 minutes. Turn out and cool on a wire tray. Serve sliced with butter.

Recipe Background

Another recipe passed on to me from my mother who used it to feed our family during the war.

Brownies

Submitted by Tony Baldry MP, Friend of Blackthorn

4 oz unsalted butter	Few drops vanilla essence
4 oz plain chocolate	3 eggs (lightly beaten)
3 oz self-raising flour	2 oz chocolate drops/chunks
8 oz soft brown sugar	

Preheat oven to 180C
Mixing bowl
Cake tin (greased and lined - I use baking parchment)

Method

Melt butter and chocolate together. Mix flour, soft brown sugar, vanilla and eggs together. Pour over chocolate mixture and mix well. Pour into tin. Put chocolate drops on top. Bake for 20-25 minutes (don't overcook – they are better slightly underdone than overdone). Cool in the tin.

Top Tip

Having melted the butter and chocolate together, you can also bung the whole lot into the Magimix and just give it a whiz until it's blended.

Butler's Bakewell Tart

Submitted by Louise and Lee Butler, Blackthorn

150 g plain flour
125 g butter (chilled and diced)
2 tsp caster sugar
1 large egg (beaten)
1 jar of strawberry/raspberry jam
200 g ground almonds

175 g caster sugar
75 g butter (soft)
5 medium eggs (beaten)
15-20 ml almond essence
Icing sugar (for dusting)
Toasted almonds (slivered to decorate)

Preheat oven to 200C
Mixing bowl
10 inch shallow pie dish
Round bladed knife

Method

To make the pastry base: sift flour and salt into a bowl. Rub in 125 g of butter until the mixture resembles fine breadcrumbs. Stir in the 2 tsp of sugar. Add large egg, stirring with a round bladed knife until the ingredients begin to stick together. Collect the mixture together and knead lightly for a few seconds to make smooth dough. Wrap in foil and leave in fridge for 30 minutes to rest. Roll out pastry on a lightly floured worktop. Use to line a

10 inch shallow pie plate. Spread a good thick layer of jam over the base and leave in the fridge to chill.

To make the filling: beat the ground almonds, sugar, butter, eggs and almond essence together in a bowl. Pour into the base and spread evenly. Bake for 35-40 minutes until filling is set (you may need to cover with foil after 30 minutes to avoid burning). Dust with icing sugar and slivered almonds. Serve warm from the oven for best results, keeps for approximately 1 week.

Top Tip

Most recipes use less almond essence but I find 15 to 20 ml is perfect to give that great almond taste. I find the best jam to use is 'Bonne Maman Raspberry Conserve', expensive but worth it. When you are checking to see if the tart is cooked it needs to feel sponge like to the touch on top, this will give it a really excellent texture and not make it dry at all. Enjoy!

Apple Cake Squares

Submitted by Nina Chadbone, Blackthorn

110 g self raising flour
1 tsp baking powder
110 g butter (or soft margarine) at room temperature
110 g caster sugar
2 large eggs

2 drops vanilla extract
2-3 apples
2-3 tsp Demerara sugar

Preheat oven to 170C
Mixing bowl
Square cake tin (lined with greaseproof paper)

Method

Sieve the flour and baking powder into a bowl and then just add all the other ingredients. Whisk the mixture together until smooth and pale, until the mixture falls off the spoon with ease. If it is a bit sticky still add a small amount of warm water until it is the right consistency. Put the mixture into a cake tin. Peel and core the apples and then slice and lay on the top. Sprinkle the Demerara sugar on top and place in the oven for 30 minutes. Leave in the tin for 30 seconds and then take out and put on a wire rack to cool.

Sticky Lemon and Poppy Seed Muffins

Submitted by Sue and Andy Sparkes, Blackthorn

400 g plain flour
1 tbsp baking powder
175 g caster sugar
3 tsp poppy seeds
284 ml buttermilk

2 beaten eggs
85 g melted butter
50 g icing sugar
Juice of 1 and grated zest of 2 lemons

Preheat oven to 200C
Mixing bowls
Muffin cases

Makes 12

Method

In a large bowl mix together the flour, baking powder, caster sugar, poppy seeds and the grated zest of a lemon. In another bowl mix together the buttermilk, beaten eggs and melted butter. Stir the mixture into the dry ingredients until just combined. Divide between 12 muffin cases and bake for 25 minutes until golden. To make the icing drizzle, mix together icing sugar and lemon zest, then gradually add lemon juice until you have a smooth, slightly runny icing, adding more juice if needed. Spoon over the cooked muffins and cool on a wire rack.

Mille Feuille

Submitted by Jenny Lamont, Blackthorn

1 pack readymade puff pastry
(rolled out and cut into 2
evenly sized rectangles)
1 punnet of raspberries/straw-
berries

1 pot whipping cream
Icing sugar (lots)
Vanilla essence

Preheat oven to 180C
Baking sheet
Mixing bowl
Piping bag

Method

Prick the pastry rectangles with a fork and bake for 15-20
minutes; then cool on a wire rack. Whip the double cream with
the vanilla essence and add some icing sugar to make a Chantilly
cream filling. On one of the cooled puff pastry sheets pipe on
the whipped cream then top with some of the fruit. Make a
coulis with the remainder of the fruit.

To do this: place the fruit in a saucepan and mash gently with
a fork, sift in the icing sugar, stirring until dissolved. When the

raspberries are heated and just simmering, pour through a sieve into a bowl, pushing the juice through with a wooden spoon. Taste, adding more sugar if desired, although the coulis should be tart; allow to cool. Pour the cooled sauce over the fresh fruit and then top with a bit more cream and the other puff pastry sheet.

For the icing: mix the icing sugar with a little water to form a white icing then put this over the top of the mille feuille, refrigerate until icing has set, about an hour. Cut the mille feuille into slices then garnish with fresh raspberries and the coulis. Yum....

Top Tip

Prepare the coulis in advance for best results.

Recipe Background

The chef at work makes these for our Thursday afternoon cake run; they soon became my favourite so I just had to have the recipe!

Lavender Scones

Submitted by Tamsin Addison, Blackthorn

225 g self raising flour
1 tsp baking powder
50 g butter (cold and cut into cubes)
75 g lavender sugar

Pinch of salt
150 ml buttermilk

Preheat oven to 220C
Mixing bowl
6 cm cake cutter
Baking tray

Makes 10-12

Method

Sift flour and baking powder into large bowl. Rub butter in lightly with fingers until mixture resembles breadcrumbs. Stir in lavender sugar and salt. Make a well in the centre of mixture. Pour in buttermilk and combine lightly to make dough. Roll out on cold surface until 2 cm thick. Cut scones from the dough. Place on a baking tray and brush tops with buttermilk. Cook for 10-15 minutes until lightly browned. Cool on a wire rack and sprinkle with extra lavender sugar and if desired lavender petals. Serve warm with home made jam.

Top Tip

To make lavender sugar: place lavender heads (Hidcote lavender recommended) in a jar of caster sugar, mix well and leave to infuse (for at least a week).

Parkin

Submitted by Eileen Iredale, Friend of Blackthorn

1 lb oatmeal
½ lb plain flour
1 lb treacle (I use half golden syrup and half treacle)
6 oz brown sugar
6 oz butter

2 tsp ground ginger
1 tsp bicarbonate of soda
½ pt of milk
2 small eggs (beaten)
Pinch of salt

Preheat oven to 150C
Large mixing bowl
Greased 8 inch square tin

Method

Melt treacle, sugar and fat together in pan. Warm milk slightly and add bicarbonate of soda. Mix dry ingredients in large bowl. Add treacle mix, milk and eggs. Pour into greased tin and bake for at least 1 hour. Allow to cool and cut into squares.

Recipe background

This is an old Yorkshire recipe traditionally served on Bonfire Night round the fire.

Jean Bannock's Almond Shortbread

Submitted by Edwin Bannock MBE, Blackthorn

12 oz plain flour
8 oz butter (not margarine)
4 oz caster sugar

4 oz blanched and halved
almonds
1 small egg (beaten)

Preheat oven to 180C
Mixing bowl
Baking sheet

Method

Sieve flour and sugar into a bowl. Beat in the butter until fully mixed. Use hands to form a smooth, silky ball with the dough. Once done, dust a baking tray with flour and place dough directly on this tray. Roll out the mixture evenly until it is approximately half an inch thick. Mark out sections to desired shapes but squares or fingers work best. Prick all over with a fork and then brush all over with the beaten egg. Place the almonds on the sections and push gently into the surface. Bake for 30-40 minutes or until a pale golden brown.

Allow to cool slightly before removing from the tray.

Enjoy and don't eat all in one go!

Recipe Background

This is a recipe handed down through my mum's family originating in Ulster and was always a treat when we were children.

Now we make it for our kids and they are just learning how to make it as well. So the recipe lives on.

Caramel Crunch Biscuits

Submitted by Susan Henderson, Blackthorn

400 g caster sugar (golden is best)
2 tbsp water

250 g butter (softened)
250 g plain flour

Preheat oven to 160C
Heavy based pan
Mixing bowl
Non-stick baking sheet (greased)
Baking tray (lined with grease proof paper)

Method

Put 150 g of the sugar into a small heavy pan with the water. Heat gently, stirring until the sugar has dissolved. Boil rapidly until the mixture begins to darken and gives off a caramel smell. Pour the caramel into the baking tray and leave until cold and brittle. When brittle break into small pieces, use food processor if you want. Cream the butter and remaining sugar together until fluffy. Mix in the crushed caramel and flour to create soft dough. Form into small balls and set on the baking tray. Bake for 12-15 minutes until golden brown. Remove from oven but leave to cool for about 5 minutes. Remove from the baking tray and leave to cool fully on a wire rack. These are lovely with a nice cuppa!

Rocky Road

Submitted by G. Mobbs, Blackthorn

125 g soft butter
200 g milk chocolate
100 g dark chocolate
(minimum 70% cocoa solids)
3 x 15 ml tbsp of golden
syrup

200 g rich tea biscuits
100 g mini marshmallows
2 tsp of icing sugar for dusting

Heavy based saucepan
Freezer bag
Foil tray (24 cm square)
Rolling pin
Spatula

Makes 24

Method

Melt the butter, chocolate and golden syrup in the pan. Make sure you keep 125 ml of the mixture to the side for later. Put the rich tea biscuits into the freezer bag and hit the bag with the end of the rolling pin. At the end you are aiming for crumbs and pieces of biscuits. Fold all the biscuit (crumbs and pieces) into the melted chocolate mixture which should be in the saucepan, then add the marshmallows. Tip the mixture into the foil tray and flatten as best as possible with a spatula. Pour the reserved 125 ml of the mixture in the foil tray and smooth the top over. Refrigerate for 2-3 hours or overnight. Once they have been refrigerated, cut into fingers, squares or however you like then dust with the icing sugar by gently pushing it through a small sieve.

Betty's Flapjack

(Known as Jenny's Flapjack in Blackthorn)

Submitted by Jenny Thompson, Blackthorn

500 g butter (salted)
2 cups sugar
2 heaped tbsp golden syrup

2 cups plain flour
4 cups porridge oats (large or
small)

Preheat oven to 180C
Large heavy bottomed non-stick saucepan
Baking tray (greased then lined)

Method

Melt butter and syrup over medium heat then add sugar stirring
until dissolved. Take off the heat and add oats and flour,
mix well. Pour into prepared tray and bake for roughly 12-15
minutes depending on oven until very lightly brown (The lighter
it is the chewier it will be, the darker it is the harder it will be!)
Put tray on cooling rack. After roughly 10 minutes mark out
pieces with sharp knife. After another 15 minutes break up the
pieces and lay out to further cool on double layers of kitchen
roll which absorbs any excess of butter.

Swedish Almond Cake

Submitted by Maya Grell, Blackthorn

300 ml flour
100 ml ground almonds
200 ml sugar
1 tbsp vanilla sugar
1 tsp baking powder
150 ml milk

1 egg
150 g melted butter
Juice of ½ a lemon
Icing sugar
Chocolate shavings

Preheat oven to 175C

Method

Mix dry ingredients. Add milk, egg, and melted butter. Mix and cook for 50-60 minutes. Top with lemon icing: mix the lemon juice and icing sugar together until it holds. Sprinkle shaved chocolate on the top if you want.

My Mormor (that's granny in Swedish) always makes this when the family gets together for tea. Tristan, my little brother, and I love it!

Gingerbread

Submitted by Morag Trilk, Blackthorn

450 g plain flour
1 tsp salt
3 tsp ground ginger
3 tsp baking powder
1 tsp bicarbonate of soda
225 g Demerara sugar

175 g butter
175 g black treacle
175 g golden syrup
300 ml milk
1 egg beaten

Preheat oven to 170C
Heavy bottomed non-stick saucepan
Mixing bowl
9 inch square cake tin (greased and lined)

Method

Put the sugar, fat, treacle and syrup in a saucepan. Warm gently
over a low heat until melted and well blended (do not boil).
Remove from heat and cool slightly, until you can hold your
hand comfortably against the side of the pan. Sift together the
flour, salt, ginger, baking powder and bicarbonate of soda in
a large mixing bowl. Mix the milk and egg into the cooled wet
ingredients. Make a well in the centre of the dry ingredients,
pour in the liquid and mix thoroughly. Turn into the tin and

bake for about 1 hour 30 minutes or until firm to touch. Turn out onto a wire rack to cool. For best flavour, store for a few days wrapped in foil before eating.

Recipe Background

I use this recipe often for cake sales and coffee mornings as it's so easy to make, a nice alternative to sponge or fairy cakes and it can be made in advance!

Pumpkin and Ginger Teabread

Submitted by Nina Chadbone, Blackthorn

175 g melted butter
140 g clear honey
1 large egg beaten
250 g raw peeled pumpkin
(coarsely grated)

100 g light muscovado sugar
350 g self-raising flour
1 tbsp ground ginger
2 tbsp Demerara sugar

Preheat oven to 180C
1.5 kg loaf tin
Mixing bowl

Method

Butter and line a loaf tin. Mix the honey, butter and egg and then stir in the pumpkin. Mix in the muscovado sugar, flour and ginger. Pour the mixture into the prepared tin and sprinkle the top with the Demerara sugar. Bake for 50-60 minutes, until risen and golden brown. Leave in the tin for 5 minutes then turn out and cool on a wire rack.

Cinnamon and Carrot Cake

Submitted by Doreen Shirley, Friend of Blackthorn

18 oz wholemeal flour
4 oz caster sugar
1 tbsp cinnamon
2 bananas (mashed)
1½ tsp baking powder
6 oz carrots (grated)

4 oz butter (melted)
4 oz cream cheese
2 tbsp apricot jam
2 oz icing sugar
1 tbsp lemon juice

Preheat oven to 170C
Mixing bowl
Loaf tin

Serves 6-8

Method

Mix together flour, cinnamon and baking powder. Combine
butter, jam and sugar together and stir into flour with bananas
and carrots. Mix well. Pour into loaf tin. Bake for 1–1¼ hours
until firm to touch. Allow to cool slightly before removing from
tin. Mix remaining ingredients together and spread over the cake
when cool.

Apple Cake

Submitted by Linda and Michael Rees, Blackthorn

340 g self raising flour
Pinch of Salt
110 g sultanas
3 eggs

225 g butter
170 g sugar
450 g cooking apples

Preheat oven to 180C
Mixing bowl
20 cm cake tin

Method

Grease and flour cake tin. Sift flour and salt. Rub in butter. Stir in sugar and sultanas. Core and dice the apples and mix in. Lightly beat the eggs and fold in. Bake in centre of the oven for 1 hour and 15 minutes. Sprinkle with sugar while still hot.

Recipe Background

This recipe is one that my sister-in-law gave me and is a family favourite. You don't need to peel the apples so preparation time is minimal.

Unusual Fruit Cake

Submitted by Margaret Golby, Friend of Blackthorn

7 oz self raising flour
1 lb sultanas
8 oz margarine
10 oz caster sugar

1 tsp vanilla essence
3 eggs
12 oz self raising flour
1 pt water

Preheat oven to 150C
Cook on hob then bake in oven
Saucepan
Mixing bowl
Cake tin (greased and lined)

Method

Simmer the sultanas in water for 10 minutes, then drain. Melt the margarine into the sultanas. Beat together the sugar, eggs and vanilla essence. Gradually add the flour and fruit and mix thoroughly. Spoon into the prepared tin and cook for 1 hour 15 minutes.

Mrs Porteous' Milk Chocolate Cake

Submitted by Susan Henderson, Blackthorn

7 oz self raising flour
8 oz caster sugar
½ tsp salt
1 oz cocoa powder
4 oz margarine
2 eggs (beaten with 5 tbsp evaporated milk)

5 tbsp water
Few drops vanilla essence
2½ oz margarine
1 tbsp cocoa
9 oz sieved icing sugar
3 tbsp hot milk
1 tbsp of vanilla essence

Preheat oven to 180C (170C in fan assisted oven)
Mixing bowl
2 cake tins (8 inch, do not use loose bottomed tins as the mixture will run out)

Method

Sieve flour, sugar, salt and cocoa. Rub in margarine. Stir in eggs, essence and liquids, beat well. Grease and flour tins, divide the mixture between them. Bake for about 30-35 minutes. When cold cover and sandwich together with milk chocolate icing. To make the chocolate icing: melt margarine, blending in cocoa then stir in icing sugar, milk and essence, beat well until smooth and thick. Serve with strawberries if in season.

Carrie's Dark Chocolate and Cherry Loaf Cake

Submitted by Carrie Kirby, Blackthorn

225 g soft unsalted butter
375 g dark muscovado sugar
2 large free range eggs (beaten)
1 tsp vanilla extract
100 g dark chocolate (melted, 90% cocoa solids works best for me)

200 g natural coloured glace cherries
1 tbsp flour for dusting
200 g plain flour
1 tsp bicarbonate of soda

Preheat oven to 190C
23 x 13 x 7cm loaf tin
Baking sheet

Makes 8-10 slices

Method

Put a baking sheet in the bottom of the oven to catch potential drips. Use parchment/silicone or paper liner as this very damp cake really needs it to come out in one piece! Cream the butter and sugar, and then add eggs and vanilla. Beat well. Next, fold in the slightly melted chocolate. Don't over beat as you want a well combined, not airy mixture. Wash and dry the cherries, chop then roll them in a little flour until well dusted. Add to the creamed chocolate buttery egg mixture. Next add the bicarbonate of soda to the flour and add the flour, alternating with the boiling water spoon by spoon. You will end up with a smooth and liquid batter. Pour this mixture into the lined loaf tin and bake for 30 minutes. Then turn down the oven temperature to 170C and cook for a further 15 minutes. The cake will be squidgy inside, don't be tempted to overcook it, as you'll lose the wonderful damp moistness of the centre! Leave the loaf tin on a rack and don't attempt to remove the cake from the tin until it's completely cooled; overnight is perfect.

Top Tip

I usually serve this cake upside down if trying to impress, because it will sink due to the wonderful, delectable rich and dense centre! Is great served with raspberries and double cream or crème fraiche!

Recipe Background

This recipe has been adapted over the years. My younger child has a dairy allergy, he can eat this cake, when made with a butter substitute, as the chocolate is so dark. The cake is a family favourite and well considered around the village too; a staple of the 'village camp!'

Five Minute Mug Cake

Submitted by Alison Webb, Blackthorn

4 tbsp flour
4 tbsp sugar
2 tbsp cocoa
1 egg
3 tbsp milk

3 tbsp oil
3 tbsp chocolate chips (optional)
Small splash of vanilla extract

Cook in microwave   Serves 4
4 large coffee mugs (microwave safe)

Method

Put the dry ingredients into a bowl, and mix well. Add the egg and mix thoroughly. Pour in the milk and oil and mix well. Add the chocolate chips (if using) and vanilla extract, and mix again. Spoon the mixture into mugs. Put mugs in the microwave (1 at a time) and cook for 3 minutes at 1000 watts. The cake will rise over the top of the mug, but don't be alarmed! Allow to cool a little, and tip out onto a plate if desired. EAT! (Each cake can serve 2 if you want to feel slightly more virtuous).

Why is this the most dangerous cake recipe in the world? Because now we are all only 5 minutes away from chocolate cake at any time of the day or night!

Auntie Polly's Sultana Cake

Submitted by Susan Henderson, Blackthorn

4 oz sugar
2 eggs
2 oz mixed peel
1 tsp baking powder
4 oz butter

8 oz self raising flour
6 oz sultanas
Milk
Salt

Preheat oven to 180C
Mixing bowl
Cake tin (greased and lined)

Method

Cream together the butter and sugar until light and fluffy. Add the egg and mix together. Gradually add the flour. Mix in the fruit. Bake in the oven for 1 hour 30 minutes or until golden.

Truffles

Submitted by Mrs Harris, Friend of Blackthorn

¼ lb margarine	2 tsp desiccated coconut
1 tin condensed milk	20 digestive biscuits
4 tsp cocoa	Vermicelli (to decorate)

Saucepan
Mixing bowl

Method

Melt the margarine in a pan. In a separate bowl crumble the biscuits and add the cocoa and coconut. Take the margarine off the heat and add milk. Mix with the biscuits (you may not need to add all the milk mixture as the biscuit mix does not want to be too wet). Roll the biscuit mix into small balls and roll in the vermicelli.

Jessie's Tablet

Submitted by Susan Henderson, Blackthorn

1 cup whole milk
2 oz butter
2 lb granulated sugar

1 tin condensed milk
1 tbsp golden syrup
Few drops of vanilla essence

Large heavy based saucepan
Baking tray

Method

Put the milk, sugar and butter into the pan. Once the butter has melted and the sugar dissolved add the condensed milk. Bring mixture slowly to the boil, stirring continuously. Add the syrup and boil gently for a further 5 minutes. Test the mixture by putting a teaspoon full into a cup of cold water, if it is firm and holding together the mixture is ready. Remove from the heat, add a few drops of vanilla essence and beat for 3-5 minutes. Pour mixture into baking tray and cool slightly, cut while still warm and allow to cool fully.

Cheese Biscuits

Submitted by Cate Court, Friend of Blackthorn

570 g wholemeal flour
4 cups of grated cheese (Red Leicester is best)

12 oz margarine (melted)
2 tsp of garlic salt/granules
1 cup of milk

Preheat oven to 170C
Mixing Bowl
Baking sheet

Method

Mix ingredients together until it becomes very elastic and easy to roll. Roll out to desired thickness and cut into shapes. Bake for about 20 minutes in a moderate oven until the edges are starting to darken, the thicker they are the more cooking they need. As they cool they will become hard and biscuit like. Keep in an airtight container and they should keep for a couple of weeks.

Sweet Things
- Jams, Chutneys and Drinks

Tomato Relish

Submitted by Jason Williams (Bicester Vets), Friend of Blackthorn

4 large tomatoes (cut into chunks)
4 medium onions (skinned and cut into chunks)
Salt
Malt vinegar (enough to cover)

1 lb white sugar
1 tbsp curry powder
1 dsp mustard powder
2 tbsp plain flour

Cook on hob
Heavy based non-stick saucepan
Sterilised jars or bottles

Method

Take tomatoes and onions, sprinkle with salt and leave covered overnight (not in a metal bowl). Next day drain off fluid through a colander. Put into a large pan, cover with malt vinegar and cook for 30 minutes. Then add sugar and stir. Blend curry powder, mustard powder and flour with some vinegar to make a paste. Add some of the warm fluid from the pan to start mixing in with the paste before mixing this into the pot. Cook for 10 minutes, stirring all the time with a wooden spoon (apparently this is important!). It will stick to the bottom if you don't keep stirring. Bottle when cooled a little. It will keep for months and gets better with time.

Recipe Background

Recipe is from my mother in Australia (and no doubt from her mother before that). Great with fried breakfast, chops and sausage/bacon butties!

Pickled Peppers

Submitted by Chris Isaacs, Blackthorn

1.5 kg peppers (red or green or mixture of both)
45 ml salt
750 ml red wine vinegar
Sealed vinegar proof jars
Saucepan

2 bay leaves
2 sprigs of thyme
2 sprigs of parsley
5 ml peppercorns

Method

Cut Peppers into halves or quarters depending on their size. Remove the seeds and core and cut into 5 mm slices. Place in a bowl and sprinkle each layer with salt. Cover and leave for 12 hours to extract moisture. Rinse the peppers well to remove the salt then drain and dry well. Place vinegar in saucepan with the remaining ingredients (tied in a muslin bag if just the flavour is required) and heat to boiling point. Place peppers into jars then strain in boiling vinegar. If desired, place herbs down the side of the jar to enhance visual look. Seal jars.

Recipe background

This recipe was passed down from my Grandmother who died aged 101!!

Weirdown Tea Time Pickle

Submitted by Becca, Dan and Moley, Blackthorn

6 cups of young cucumbers
1 lb small white onions
1 green pepper
¼ cup of salt
Syrup mixture:
2 cups of brown sugar

1 tbsp of mustard seed
½ tsp of turmeric
½ tsp celery seed
¼ tsp of ground clove
2 cups of cider vinegar

Cook on hob
Large bowl
Large saucepan
Sterilised jam jars

Method

Wash the cucumbers (but don't peel) and slice thinly. Peel and slice the onions. Deseed and shred the pepper. Mix the vegetables in a large bowl; add the salt, cover and leave to stand for a minimum of 3 hours (we normally leave it overnight with no problem). Drain thoroughly in a colander, rinsing under cold water. Drain again then add to the hot syrup.

For the hot syrup: mix all syrup ingredients together and bring slowly to boiling point and boil for 5 minutes. Heat to just below boiling stirring every now and then. Allow to cool and put in sterilised jars.

Recipe Background

This pickle has been made at Weirdown since the family first came to Blackthorn in 1976 and originally comes from a cookery book brought back from Canada in 1950 by my parents.

Randal's Chutney

Submitted by Randal Rue, Blackthorn

10 large cooking apples
8 large onions
20 tomatoes (preferably green)
4 peppers
1 kg stoned dates
20 cm fresh root ginger
5 green (mild) chillies
10 red (hot) chillies

3 tsp mustard powder
40 crushed black pepper-corns
100 g tomato puree
12 cloves of garlic
1 tsp salt
1.7 ltr malt vinegar
2 kg Demerara Sugar

Cook on hob
Heavy bottomed non-stick saucepan
20 sterilised jars

Method

Peel the apples, onions, tomatoes, ginger, and garlic. Remove the apple cores. Chop all the fruit and spices and place in pan. Add about half the vinegar and sugar. Simmer over a low heat all day, stirring regularly. Leave to cool overnight. Next day simmer again, adding the rest of the sugar and vinegar to taste. After a few hours stirring it will be ready to bottle whilst still hot.

Top Tip

These quantities are approximate, and will depend on fruit available, and how spicy you like your chutney.

Recipe Background

This is a traditional family recipe given to me by mother, Dame Rosemary Rue, but I also remember my grandmother and aunt making it. I have modernised it with spices I bring back from islands in the Indian Ocean. I hope you enjoy it.

Marrow and Ginger Jam

Submitted by Linda Hendren, Friend of Blackthorn

6 lb prepared marrow
(peeled and deseeded)
2 oz root ginger

Juice and grated rind of 4
lemons
6 lb sugar

Cook on hob
Heavy bottomed non-stick saucepan
Muslin bag
Sterilised jars

Method

Cut the marrow flesh into tiny cubes and steam until tender.
Bruise the ginger, tie in a muslin bag and place in the pan with
the steamed marrow and the juice and rind of lemons. Bring to
the boil, stir in the sugar until it has dissolved, then boil rapidly
to setting point. Test for setting. Pot at once and allow to cool
before sealing the jars.

Plum Chutney

Submitted by Sandie Stevenson, Blackthorn

2½ lb plums (stoned, skinned and chopped)
1 lb onions (finely chopped)
2 lb apples (peeled, cored and chopped)
1½ pt malt vinegar

½ g salt
1 lb brown sugar
2 tsp cloves
2 tsp all spice
2 tsp black pepper corns
1 small piece of root ginger

Cook on hob
Heavy bottomed non-stick saucepan
Sterilised jars

Method

To make spiced vinegar: Mix together the brown sugar, ½ pt of the vinegar and all the spices in a large saucepan and bring to the boil. Simmer for 5 minutes. Infuse and cool for 30 minutes then strain. Put the prepared fruit and onion into a pan with the salt and the rest of the vinegar and simmer till soft. Add the spiced vinegar and simmer for 2 hours. Pour into jam jars and allow to cool, seal and do not use for 2 months.

Crab Apple and Ginger Jelly

Submitted by Keith and Caroline Crampton, Blackthorn

Crab apples	Lemons
Water	Root ginger
Sugar	

Cook on hob
Heavy bottomed non-stick saucepan
Sterilised jars
Jelly bag

Method

Wash crab apples, remove any blemishes and cut in half. Place in preserving pan or similar, add an inch or so of root ginger per pan of crab apples, and cover with water. Bring to boil and simmer until reduced to soft pulp. Strain through a jelly bag overnight (DO NOT squeeze otherwise jelly will be cloudy) Measure the juice and return to pan. Add 1 lb of sugar and the pared rind of a half lemon to each 1 pt of crab apple juice. Bring to boil slowly until all sugar has dissolved. Boil rapidly until setting point is reached (approximately 15 minutes). Pour into warmed jars (removing lemon rind) and cover as for jam.

Mincemeat

(something for Christmas)

Submitted by Liz Mobbs, Blackthorn

1 lb cooking apples
8 oz shredded suet
8 oz sultanas
8 oz currants
8 oz whole mixed peel
12 oz raisins
12 oz soft dark brown sugar
Grated rind and juice of
2 oranges

Grated rind and juice of
2 lemons
2 oz flaked almonds
4 tsp of mixed spice
½ tsp of ground cinnamon
½ tsp grated nutmeg
6 tbsp of brandy
4 glace cherries

Cook on hob
Heavy bottomed non-stick saucepan
Large bowl
6–8 jam jars with lids (I use 'Bonne Maman' jars because they make pretty pots to give away as gifts)
Wax discs

Method

Mix all the ingredients together very thoroughly in a large bowl, except for the brandy. Leave it to stand overnight, making sure you cover it with a cloth. When you go back to it, stir in the brandy and spoon into clean dry jars (if you want to sterilise the jars you can). Cover with wax discs and seal.

Recipe Background

We make this every year at least six weeks before Christmas, so it has time to mature before being made into mince pies. Once you have tasted your own home made mincemeat, you won't want anything else!

Blackthorn Rhubarb and Date Chutney

Submitted by David Wood, Blackthorn

1lb rhubarb
1 medium onion
8 oz stoned dates
1 level tsp salt

1 level tsp ground ginger
1 level tsp cayenne pepper
¾ pint malt vinegar

Cook on hob
Large saucepan or casserole dish
Sterilised jam jars

Makes 3-4 jam jars

Method

Slice the rhubarb into 1 inch strips. Chop the onion and dates roughly. Put all ingredients in the saucepan and bring to the boil gently on the hob. Simmer uncovered for about an hour. Rhubarb loses a lot of water when boiled so strain in a sieve when the mixture has cooled until it is the right consistency for chutney.

Strawberry and Orange Jam

Submitted by Naomi Karslake, Blackthorn

4 lb strawberries
The juice and grated rind of
3 oranges
4 lb preserving sugar
1 oz butter

Cook on hob
Heavy bottomed non-stick saucepan
Sterilised jam jars (enough for 6 lb)

Method

Remove the strawberry stalks and cut in half. Put into pan
along with the orange rind and juice. Put the pan over a low
heat, cover and simmer for 15 minutes; until the strawberries
are really soft. Add the sugar and stir until all the sugar has
dissolved. Bring the mixture to a rolling boil and then boil
rapidly for a further 10 minutes. To test to see if the jam has set
put a tsp of the mixture onto a cold plate, allow to cool slightly
the top layer should wrinkle when touched, keep boiling until
this consistency is achieved, test every couple of minutes.

Stir in the butter; this will remove any scum that has formed. Leave to cool for 10 minutes then pour into warmed jars. Allow jam to fully cool and set then seal and label.

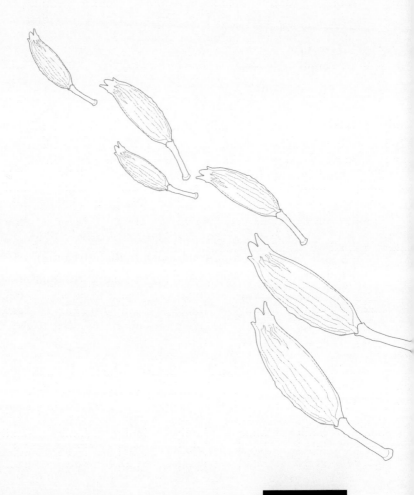

Sandie's Blackthorn Sangria

Submitted by Sandie Stevenson, Blackthorn

26 fl oz dry red wine
3 oz sugar
1/3 cup Cointreau
1 ltr orange juice
Lemon, lime and orange
slices

Large jug/pitcher

Method

Combine all ingredients and chill in the refrigerator overnight.
Pour into chilled glasses and serve. Great with tapas as some of
you already know!

Grandma Burden's Elderflower Champagne

Submitted by Sue Burden, Blackthorn

4 large heads of elderflower
1 lemon (juice and rind)
2 tbsp white wine vinegar
1½ lb granulated sugar
8 pt water

Sterilised jars or bottles

Method

Put all the ingredients into a large container and cover with the water. Stir well, cover and leave for 24 hours. Strain through a sieve into sterilised bottles or jars and leave in a cool place for 2-3 weeks. Store up to 3 months.

Recipe Background

This is light and only very slightly alcoholic (5%) and has a wonderful taste. Elderflowers are hand picked from the hedgerow. Ideal for Christmas!

Cider Toddy

Submitted by Hilary Wright, Blackthorn

½ pint of dry cider
1 piece of root ginger
1 strip of lemon rind
1 tbsp of clear honey

Heat on hob
Saucepan

Method

Put cider, ginger and lemon rind into a pan. Heat until hot but not boiling. Stir in the honey. Strain into a warmed glass.

Recipe Background

This is an old wartime recipe. This makes a warming drink to enjoy on a cold winters night. Very reviving.

Plum Smoothie

Submitted by Nick Crutch, Friend of Blackthorn

2 chopped plums
1 chopped banana
½ tsp powdered ginger
Seeds of ½ vanilla pod
½ tbsp runny honey

100 ml freshly squeezed
orange juice (with zest)
85 ml low fat bio yoghurt
½ handful of ice

Blender

Serves 1

Method

Blend all ingredients (except the ginger) until smooth. Serve with ginger sprinkled on top.

Recipe Background

I use this as a mid morning meal. The mixture of fruits means that you get varying levels of energy release due to different glycaemic index values. There is a high sugar content, mainly due to the banana. However bananas are a good source of vitamin C, vitamin B6 and magnesium.

Sue's Berry Spiced Gin

Submitted by Sue Burden, Blackthorn

375 g mixed frozen berries
1 cinnamon stick
2.5 cm piece of root ginger
4 cloves
1 lemon (halved)

1 orange (halved)
300 g golden caster sugar
1 ltr of gin
Water (as per method)

Saucepans
Mixing bowl
Sterilised bottles or jars

Method

Put frozen berries, cinnamon, ginger, cloves, lemon and orange into a pan with 300 ml water. Simmer for 5 minutes, crushing the fruit with back of spoon, then leave to cool. Make syrup by putting sugar in a pan with 450 ml water, bring to boil and bubble for 5 minutes, then leave to cool. In a large bowl mix together the berry mixture, syrup and gin. Cover with cling film and put in a cool dark place for a week, stirring occasionally. After one week the gin will have infused, carefully strain through a sieve lined with kitchen paper. Then decant into sterilised bottles. Keep in a cool dark place for up to 3 months.

Recipe Background

This truly is a Christmas cracker and a great alternative to an after dinner liqueur. It can also be served over ice or with warmed apple juice and it gives mulled wine a big kick. A great present too! Made last Christmas and was a great hit.

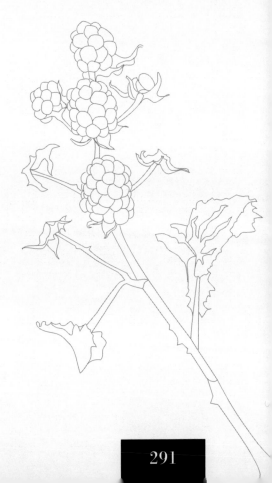

Celebrity
Chef's
Recipe

Steamed Mussels with Tomato and Tarragon

Submitted by Rick Stein, Friend of Blackthorn

1 kg mussels
30 ml extra virgin olive oil
30 ml dry white wine
60 g tomatoes (peeled, deseeded and finely chopped)

5 g French tarragon (finely chopped)
2 cloves garlic (finely chopped)
30 g unsalted butter

Method

Make sure the mussels are tightly closed. If they are fresh-farmed ones there is no need to wash them, but if they are showing any signs of grit or sand wash them in copious amounts of cold water. Take a large saucepan, add the olive oil and garlic and soften over a medium heat for about a minute. Add the mussels, turn up the heat and add the white wine. Put a lid

The Seafood Restaurant
riversidepadstowcornwallPL288BY
telephone:01841 532700 fax:01841 532942
email:reservations@rickstein.com

on the pan and cook for a few minutes until all the shells have opened, but only just. Stir the shells once or twice during the cooking to distribute them evenly.
Remove and pour through a colander set over a bowl.

Keep the mussels warm while you transfer the liquor to a pan, heat until boiling, whisk in the butter then add the tomato and tarragon. Check the seasoning; it's always a good idea to leave seasoning to the end with shellfish because you never know how salty they are going to be, then add salt if necessary and freshly ground black pepper.

Add the mussels back into the pan. Serve with plenty of crusty bread or alternatively with a mound of al dente linguine pasta.

Rick Stein

Local Chefs' Suggested Menus

Artizian Wargrave

Starter - Gazpacho

1 kg ripe plum tomatoes
500 g cucumber
250 g red pepper
1 clove garlic
100 ml sherry vinegar
50 ml white wine vinegar
400 ml olive oil

200 g of bread
Salt
Red pepper, green pepper,
tomato (deseeded and
peeled), onion, cucumber
(All diced for garnish)
Fried croutons

Food processor

Serves 8

Method

Place all the vegetables in a food processor with a little salt and blitz. Place the bread to soak in cold water until soft. Add half the vinegar to the mixture and the soaked bread. Slowly add half of the olive oil to start emulsifying the mixture. Then add the rest of the vinegar (this depends on the strength that you want). Add the rest of the olive oil and emulsify. Pass through a sieve. Season and chill. (Depending on the mixture you can correct flavours by adding more olive oil or vinegar to the final mix).

Main - Grilled Mackerel with Sake

4 x 8 oz mackerel
(gutted and trimmed)
1 cucumber (finely sliced)
3 tbsp rice wine vinegar
2 tbsp pickled ginger
Mizuna/rocket leaves
1 tbsp toasted sesame seeds

For the sake glaze:
3 tbsp sake
½ tsp paprika
3 tbsp mirin
¼ tsp wasabi
1 tbsp rice wine vinegar
2 tbsp dark soy sauce
1 tsp sugar

Preheat the grill (highest setting)
Shallow dish

Serves 4

Method

Rinse the mackerel under running cold water and dry with
absorbent paper. Cut 6-8 diagonal slashes in each side of the
mackerel, right through to the bone. Put the fish into a shallow
dish. Mix together the ingredients for the glaze and spoon half
of it over the fish. Put the remainder in a small bowl. Thinly
slice the cucumber and arrange, overlapping on a large plate.
Sprinkle with the rice wine vinegar and pickled ginger, pile the
mizuna/rocket leaves on top. Cover and refrigerate whilst you
cook the fish. Put the mackerel onto a grill tray and pour any
juices over the top. Grill for 4-5 minutes on each side, basting
frequently with the remaining marinade, until the fish is cooked
(it should be opaque and firm). When all the basting glaze is
used up and the fish is a good colour, sprinkle with the sesame
seeds and return to the grill for a further 30 seconds. Lift the fish
from the grill and arrange on a large serving platter. Serve the
cucumber and mizuna salad separately.

Dessert - Double Ginger Cake

250 g self raising flour
2 tbsp syrup
(from the ginger jar)
2 level tsp ground ginger
55 g stem ginger (in syrup)
½ tsp ground cinnamon
2 heaped tbsp sultanas

1 level tsp bicarbonate of soda
125 g butter
Pinch salt
125 g dark muscavado sugar
200 g golden syrup
2 eggs large
240 ml milk

Preheat oven to 180C
Small saucepan
Mixing bowl
22 cm cake tin (greased and lined)

Serves 4

Method

Sieve the flour with the ginger, cinnamon, bicarbonate of soda
and salt. Put the golden syrup and ginger syrup and butter into a
small saucepan and warm over a low heat. Dice the ginger finely
then add to the pan with the sultanas and sugar. Let the mixture
bubble for a minute and stir. Break eggs into a bowl, pour in the
milk and beat gently. Remove the butter and sugar mixture from
the heat and pour into the flour, stirring smoothly with a large
metal spoon. Mix in the milk and eggs. The mixture should be
sloppy with no trace of flour. Scoop the mixture into the lined
cake tin and bake for 35-40 minutes or until a skewer when
inserted comes out clean. This cake can be wrapped in foil and
allowed to mature for a couple of days.

Arzoo Bicester

Starter - Chicken Kupita

1 kg boneless minced chicken
½ ltr of vegetable cooking oil
2 medium sized onions (finely chopped)
3 tsp ginger and garlic paste
A large handful of coriander leaves

1 tsp of turmeric powder
1 tbsp of garammasla powder
2 tbsp of red chilli powder
1 tbsp of ground coriander
1 tsp of ground cumin powder
Salt

Cook on hob
Frying pan/deep fat fryer

Method

To make the marinade: mix the turmeric, garammasla, chilli, coriander and cumin powders together and add salt to taste. Add the minced chicken and other ingredients and mix well, then marinate for 1 hour. Once marinated, roll the chicken mix into golf ball sized pieces. Put the vegetable oil in a pan or fryer, bring to the boil then add the chicken balls. Once fried, serve on a plate with salad and some mint sauce.

Main - Halibut Lazizz

2 halibut steaks
50 ml vegetable oil
2 medium onions (finely chopped)
3 tsp of chopped garlic
1 tsp of dried fenugreek leaves
1 tbsp of tomato puree

3 tbsp of mixed curry powder
1 fresh tomato (chopped into quarters)
2 mixed peppers (deseeded and sliced)
Salt (to taste)
1 tbsp of mixed curry powder
2 tsp of garlic paste

Cook on hob
Frying pan

Method

Mix 1 tbsp of curry powder and the garlic paste in a bowl then add the two halibut steaks and rub the marinade on. Then heat a pan and add enough vegetable oil to pan fry. Fry halibut then put aside while making the sauce.

In the same pan add the rest of the vegetable oil with the chopped garlic, salt and the chopped onion cook till golden. Then add the fenugreek leaves, tomato puree and 3 tbsp of mixed curry powder, stir, then add a quarter pint of water. Add halibut steaks along with fresh tomatoes and mixed peppers.

Dennis Bicester

Starter - Potato Borek

5 sheets filo pastry
4 yellow potatoes
(boiled and mashed)
1 medium sized onion (thinly
sliced)
¼ cup feta cheese (crumbled)

2 tbsp butter
½ tsp ground red pepper
Salt and pepper
1 egg yolk
1 tsp nigella seeds

Preheat oven to 200C
Oven tray (covered with grease proof paper)

Method

Sauté the onion with butter. Add in the warm mashed potatoes, feta cheese and red pepper, then mix. Season to taste. Place two sheets of pastry on top of each other on the counter and position them vertically. Cut them into four strips from top to bottom. Put some of the potato filling on the bottom side of each sheet. Leave some space around all ends. Then roll up each one, do not squeeze! Soak the open end in water and close it up. Fold another sheet of pastry around. Place on tray and arrange the Borek with the folded side facing down. Brush the tops with egg yolk and sprinkle some nigella seeds all over. Bake for 15-18 minutes until the tops take a golden colour.

Main - Spinach Stuffed Chicken Breast

2 small size chicken breasts
(skinless, boneless and
flattened by a mallet)
Salt and pepper
1 tbsp butter
1 small onion (finely sliced)
1 garlic clove (chopped)
3 large mushrooms (sliced)
½ cup chopped spinach
(squeezed)

¾ cup feta cheese (crumbled)
1 tsp crushed red pepper
1 tbsp butter (melted)
¼ cup sesame seeds
1 pinch red pepper
2 tbsp butter (for frying)
¼ cup sunflower oil
(for frying)

Cook on hob
Heavy based non-stick frying pan

Method

To prepare the filling: sauté the onion with butter and salt for
a few minutes in a pan. Add the garlic and sauté until the smell
of garlic comes out. Add the mushrooms and sauté for about
5 minutes. Add the spinach, ½ tsp red pepper, salt and pepper
and turn the heat off. When it has cooled down add feta cheese
and toss. Season the chicken breasts with salt and pepper.
Divide and spread the filling equally over the surface of the
chicken breasts and fold. Brush the chicken with melted butter.
Mix the rest of the red pepper and sesame seeds on a plate and
cover the stuffed breasts with the sesame seed mixture. Heat the
sun flower oil and butter in the frying pan. Fry the chicken on
both sides over a low-medium heat.

Dessert - Noah's Pudding

1 cup barley
1 cup white kidney beans
(washed and drained)
1 cup chickpeas (washed and
drained)
1 cup sugar
1 tsp vanilla extract
10 cups water

10 dry apricots (soaked in
water overnight, cut into
pieces)
10 dry figs (cut in pieces)
½ cup raisins
¼ cup crumbled walnuts (to
garnish)

Cook on hob
Large cooking pot

Serves 4

Method

Put 4 cups of water in a large pot along with the barley and
bring to the boil on high heat. As soon as it boils, turn it down
to medium-low heat and cook for about half an hour. Add the
beans, chickpeas, vanilla, apricots, raisins, figs, sugar and 6 cups
of hot water. Cook for about 45 minutes on medium-low heat,
stirring occasionally. Pour into a large serving bowl and let it
cool. Keep Noah's Pudding refrigerated. When serving, garnish
with crumbled walnuts.

*5000 years ago in Mesopotamia, Noah was King of the city Shuruppak. His
was a trade empire, and he built a large trading ship. At that time, there was a raging
flood and rainstorm. He and his family loaded animals, grain, fruit and beer onboard.
The rain continued for 40 days. Afterwards there was no land in sight for 7 days. They
ran out of drinking water and since the sea was salty, they had to resort to drinking
beer. They eventually landed on Mount Ararat. The old saying goes that Noah's
food was about to run out. He mixed and cooked all that he had left. The result
became known as "Noah's Pudding". This recipe is one of the oldest and best known
desserts of Turkish Cuisine. Its original name is "Asure". When we cook Asure, it is
traditional to give some away to friends and family. Turkish people love Asure and
there is even an Asure Month.*

Five Arrows Waddesdon

Main - Crispy Pork Belly

1 small de-boned pork belly
(ask your butcher to do this!)
2 large onions
1 bulb of garlic
4 large peeled waxy potatoes
(Desiree)

2 Granny Smith apples
Sugar
2 pt water

Preheat oven to 200C for 20 minutes then turn down to 110C
Large roasting tray

Method

Peel onions and cut into halves. Slice garlic bulb through
middle. Slice peeled potatoes into 2 cm slices. Put sliced garlic,
onions and potatoes into the centre of the roasting tray to form
a 'trivet' (like a platform) to place the pork on. Salt the belly skin
liberally and then place onto the trivet (skin side up). Add water
into the roasting tin. Put into a preheated oven and cook for 20
minutes or until the skin begins to crackle then turn the oven
down and cook for 4-5 hours checking every hour that the tray
does not dry out. If it looks dry add 1 more pint of water. When
cooked, use a sharp knife cut into 4 even portions. Put the
potatoes and onions onto the plate with the belly on top.
Drain off the fat from the roasting tray keeping the roasting

juices to use as sauce. Peel the apples and cut into halves and cover in sugar. Put the apples on a tray under a grill until golden brown. Add the apples to the plates. Now eat!

Dessert - Honeycomb Ice Cream

100 g golden syrup
200 g caster sugar
¾ tsp bicarbonate of soda
1.2 ltr double cream whipped
1 tin condensed milk

Heavy bottomed non-stick saucepan
2 ltr freezable container
Silicone based rectangular tray (lined with grease proof paper)

Method

Whip the cream until thick. Then mix in the condensed milk. Melt the sugar and golden syrup over a medium heat, until a light mahogany brown colour, and then take off the heat. Carefully whisk the bicarbonate of soda into the caramel mixture taking extra care because it will froth up a great deal when first added. When mixed in pour the honeycomb mixture into the tray. When it has cooled down take out of the tray and break into small pieces. Add all the pieces to the cream and condensed milk and mix together. Put the mixture into a container and freeze for at least 6 hours.

Top Tip

When melting the sugar and golden syrup together be careful not to take your eye off the pan at all as it can burn very easily!

Rigoletto Middleton Stoney

Starter - Taglierini Allo Scglio

250 g taglierini all'uovo pasta (De Ceco)
Four Cornish king scallops
8 good size king prawns
20 mussels
1 red pepper (skinned and finely chopped)
1/2 onion (skinned and finely chopped)

Cook on hob
Flat bottomed pan

1 lemon (non-waxed)
2 cloves of garlic (finely chopped)
50 g of cherry tomatoes (washed and quartered)
10 cl of virgin Italian olive oil
75 ml dry white wine
Flat leaf parsley (to garnish)

Serves 4

Method

Put 2 ltr of salted water in a pan and heat. Put olive oil in flat bottomed pan, warm the oil and put in the onion. Cook until the onion turns translucent and soft but not brown. Then add the garlic and the red peppers. Cook for a further 5 minutes on a low heat, the peppers will be ready when they start to go soft. Meanwhile clean the mussels, scallops and peel and head the prawns. Put the mussels and the prawns in the pan with the peppers and add wine and the cherry tomatoes. Let this cook for 5-6 minutes covering the pan with a lid, turn up the gas so it is moderately lively. When the mussels have opened you know they are cooked (do not try to eat one which has not opened). While you are continuing to cook the sauce, take the scallops and slice them in two. Now before you cook the pasta, put the sliced scallops into the pan with the mussels and season with salt and black pepper. Put the lid back on and turn the heat off (the warmth from the sauce will cook the scallops). Now the salted water in your pot should be boiling and ready to cook the taglierini all'uovo. It normally only takes around three minutes to cook this pasta or just follow the instructions on the packet. By the time the pasta is cooked and drained the scallops will be cooked and the sauce ready to mix with the pasta. Garnish with chopped flat leaf parsley and the grated zest of half the lemon.

Main - Rigoletto Roast Beef

600 g of top side
375 ml of good red wine
2 whole red onions
2 carrots
Half a head of celery

Seasoning, (sage, rosemary, bay leaf, mixed pepper corns and sea salt)
Cognac

Preheat oven to 150C
Large frying pan
Large container
Baking tray

Method

Firstly you will need to create a marinade: peel and coarsely chop the onions, carrots and the celery head, put in a large container with the wine, sea salt and all the herbs. Place the beef in the marinade and leave for up to two days and no less than 6 hours (the meat must be kept at 6-8C).

When it is ready, take the meat out and fry it in a hot pan quickly making sure all of the meat is browned. Flame it with cognac and take it off the heat. Strain the vegetables and pan fry with olive oil on a very low heat. When the vegetables are almost caramelised remove them from the heat. Place the vegetables, the brine and the meat into a baking tray (the juice must be 2 cm up the side of the meat when placed in the tray). Cover the whole tray with foil and cook for 4 hours. When the meat is nice and tender, remove the meat from the tray and let it rest. Blend the juice and vegetables and then strain to form the sauce. Cut and serve.

Dessert - Crème Caramel (Budino)

150 g of white sugar
20 ml of water
60 ml of milk
5 medium eggs

100 g of custard sugar
1 vanilla pod
One half of lemon peel
One quarter of orange peel

Preheat oven to 150C
4 x 20 ml ramekins
Heavy bottomed non-stick saucepan

Method

First you need to make the caramel: put the white sugar and water into a pan and cook over a medium heat until it is a medium dark brown colour. Pour this out into the ramekins, leave these on the side to cool down and go solid.

Now you need to make the custard: take the vanilla pod and slice down its length, open it and take the seeds out. Once you have done this chop it finely.

Put the milk, vanilla pod, orange and lemon peel in a pan and place it on the heat. Cook until it is almost at boiling point. Take all the eggs and mix in a bowl with the sugar, whisk until it has a little foam. When the milk is ready mix and whisk together. Then strain it through a fine strainer and put it in the ramekins. Place the now full ramekins into a baking tray and add cold water (water must be up to 5 mm away from the top of the ramekins) Place in the oven for about 40-45 minutes. Before you eat it you must allow it to cool down in the fridge this will allow the caramel at the bottom of the dish to liquefy and give you more sauce.

Recipe Background

This very simple dish when done correctly is still one of the greats. This little recipe of mine is my pride and joy, because it is simple and any one can do it. But to make a great example of it you must be precise, detailed and in this case follow the recipe!

Taste of Italy Brackley

Starter - Stuffed Mushrooms

8 large flat mushrooms
12 small mushrooms
1 tbsp butter
1 shallot/onion (finely chopped)
1 garlic clove (finely chopped)
Glass white wine

1 cup grated Parmesan cheese
1 cup mozzarella cheese
2 cups breadcrumbs
1 egg beaten
3 tbsp cream
2 tsp wild mushroom mix
1 tbsp truffle oil

Preheat the oven to 150C
Food processor
Lightly oiled baking tray

Method

Place the stalks of the flat mushrooms, the button mushrooms, the shallot and the garlic into a food processor and finely chop. Heat the butter in a frying pan and add the mushroom mixture, cook for a few minutes. Add the wine and cook for a few more minutes. Remove from the heat and place in a bowl and add the Parmesan cheese, breadcrumbs, egg, cream, wild mushroom mix, truffle oil and salt and pepper and mix together. Place the mushrooms on a baking tray and stuff with the filling. Sprinkle with the, mozzarella cheese and bake for 12 minutes.

Main - Turkey Milanese

Thin slices of turkey breast   Egg
Flour   Olive oil

Cook on hob
Chopping board
2 flat bottomed dishes
Frying pan

Method

Break eggs into one of the dishes and mix together. Put flour
into the other. Flour the chopping board. Dip the turkey first in
the flour, then into the egg, and then in the flour again ensuring
that each time the turkey is well coated. Lie on the board and
continue with the other pieces. When all are done pour olive oil
into a frying pan and heat gently, place the turkey fillets into the
pan and fry until cooked on one side, turn over and repeat the
process. Top up the oil if necessary. When cooked place on a
plate and sprinkle with salt, serve with lemon wedges.

Top Tip

You may have to add more olive oil to the pan. A pan normally
fits three to four pieces of turkey. Always use fresh olive oil for
each batch of turkey wiping out the pan before using again. One
cannot imagine how good these simple turkey steaks taste, serve
with a simple salad and some fries and you have an amazingly
easy delicious supper. Cook a few extra and they are great in
Ciabatta bread for lunch the next day.

The Angel Long Crendon

Starter - Twice Baked Cheese Soufflé

40 g plain flour
40 g butter
290 ml milk
3 eggs (separated)
130 g cheese (grated)

Preheat oven to 160C
Large saucepan
6 soufflé moulds (buttered and coated with semolina, then chilled)

Method

Melt the butter in a pan slowly. Take off the heat and add the flour. Mix together until sandy in texture. Put back on the heat and slowly add the milk then add the cheese. Stir and make sure there are no lumps. Leave on the side to cool for about 30 minutes. Once cooled, add the egg yolks beat until smooth. Whisk the egg whites until soft peaks form then gently fold into the mix. ¾ fill the moulds with the mix. Cook for approx 1 hour or until the top has started to brown. Leave to cool and reheat when needed. Serve with a cream cheese sauce.

Main - Fillet of Sea Bass, with Sweet Chilli Dressing

2 tbsp finely chopped garlic
2 large red chillies
(finely chopped)
2 tbsp olive oil
2 tbsp palm sugar/muscovado
3 tbsp Thai fish sauce
(nam pla)
2 tbsp lemon juice
1 tbsp water

2 x 600-800 g sea bass or guilt
head bream (filleted scaled
and pin boned)
25 g unsalted butter
(for cooking)
Olive oil and seasoning
4 shallots (sliced)
2 cloves garlic (thinly sliced)
50 g cashew nuts
25 g fresh basil leaves

Cook on hob
Heavy based non-stick frying pan

Serves 4

Method

To make the sauce: pound together the garlic and chillies in
a pestle and mortar until it forms a course paste. Heat the oil
in a small pan and add the garlic and chilli paste and fry for 1
minute. Stir in the palm sugar, fish sauce, water and lemon juice,
then bring to a simmer and keep warm. Next, lay the fillets of
sea bass in seasoned olive oil. Heat frying pan until very hot
add the unsalted butter to the pan then immediately add the sea
bass fillets skin side down (the oil on the fish should stop the
butter from burning). Cook on a high heat until the skin starts to
crisp at the sides (approximately 2-3 minutes). Turn the fillets
over and remove the pan from the heat. Leave off the heat for
a further 2-3 minutes then remove the fish and set aside (keep
warm).

To make the garnish: return the frying pan to the heat add the garlic shallots cashew nuts and fry for 2 minutes. Add the basil leaves and remove from the heat. Present the sea bass fillets on a bed of char-grilled vegetables skin side up drizzle with the sweet chilli sauce and garnish with the fried garlic, shallots and basil leaves.

Dessert - Fallen Angel Chocolate Brownie

12 oz plain chocolate
8 oz butter
2 tsp instant coffee
2 tbsp hot water
3 eggs

8 oz caster sugar
1 tsp vanilla essence
6 oz self raising flour
8 oz plain choc chips

Preheat oven to 190C
10 inch square cake tin (greased and lined)

Method

Melt the chocolate slowly in a bowl with the butter over a pan of hot water, stirring occasionally. Dissolve the coffee in the water. In another bowl, mix together the coffee, eggs, sugar and the vanilla essence. Gradually beat in the chocolate mixture. Fold in the flour, and then the chocolate chips, pour mixture into prepared tin. Bake for about 40-45 minutes or until firm to the touch and a dull crust has formed. Leave to cool in the tin and cut into squares when cold.

Top Tip

6 oz of chopped walnut pieces can be added if wanted.

The Nut Tree Murcott

Starter - Chicken Liver Parfait

4 shallots (peeled and sliced)
1 garlic clove (peeled but whole)
1 sprig of thyme
200 ml port

200 ml brandy
200 ml Madeira
1 kg butter (4 x 250 g blocks)
1 kg chicken livers
13 eggs

Preheat oven to 130C
Heavy bottomed non-stick saucepan
Prepare two terrine moulds using oil and cling film and a bain-marie for each

Makes 2 terrines

Method

Reduce the shallots, garlic, port, brandy and Madeira in a pan until there is almost no liquid. Make sure not to burn the shallots and garlic. Melt the butter in a pan and keep to one side. Crack eggs into a bowl, cover and bring to room temperature. Make sure that the chicken livers are at just above room temperature. In a blender, blend the chicken livers, eggs and the reduction together. Pour the melted butter into the chicken mix and mix thoroughly. Fill your terrine moulds with the mixture, making sure to smooth the mixture into the corners. Immediately put the terrines into the oven and cook for 30-35 minutes. The terrine should be firm and the core temperature should be 65C. Remove from the oven and leave to stand in the bain-marie for 30 minutes. Chill in the fridge until required. The terrine will keep for up to 5 days.

Main - Olive Oil Poached Halibut

4 filets of halibut (180 g each)
200 g Arborio risotto rice
1 pt light chicken stock
1 glass white wine
Extra virgin olive oil
1 tbsp each chopped chives,

chervil, tarragon, parsley, dill
and shallot
2 tbsp grated Parmesan
2 tbsp chopped sage

Preheat oven to 150C
Non-stick pan
Deep pan suitable for oven and hob

Method

To make the risotto: Place a pan on the stove to heat, with a little olive oil. Add shallots and begin to sweat, add risotto rice and continue to sweat until texture is sandy. Add white wine and cook until reduced, slowly pour in chicken stock and cook until risotto is al dente. Risotto will take approximately 21 minutes so meanwhile begin on the halibut.

Place oil in a deep pan, with sage to enhance flavour. Season your fish with both salt and pepper; submerge into olive oil and place tray in preheated oven. Fish will take around 12-13 minutes; you are looking for a flaky texture.

Back to the risotto, add herbs and small amount of butter, finish cooking, and add Parmesan and season. Leave to rest for 2-3 minutes and all will be ready to serve. Garnish plate with micro cress such as red amaranth and chervil.

Dessert - Sticky Toffee Pudding

500 g dates
750 ml warm water
300 g unsalted butter
750 g soft dark brown sugar

10 whole eggs
900 g plain flour
6 tsp bicarbonate of soda

Preheat oven to 180C
Saucepan
Blender
Baking tray

Method

Boil dates in warm water on the stove until dates are soft. Place dates and water in blender and blitz until pureed. Soften butter in microwave and blitz with brown sugar and whole eggs. Mix the pureed dates with the butter, sugar and egg mixture. Add the bicarbonate of soda to the flour and fold date mixture through. Finally give it a quick whisk to ensure it's completely mixed. Pour into tray and put into the oven. Check with knife to see if it's cooked, after 30 minutes.

The Pheasant Brill

Starter - Spinach and Parmesan Soufflé

4 oz raw sliced spinach
2½ oz plain flour
6 eggs (separated)
3 oz butter
Salt and pepper

1 pt milk
½ onion (finely chopped)
Pinch of cayenne pepper
Pinch of nutmeg

Preheat oven to 200C
6 Ramekin dishes (buttered and lined with grease proof paper)
or large oven proof dish
Whisk
Roasting tin

Method

Add the onion, cayenne pepper and nutmeg to the milk and
boil. Make a roux with the flour and butter and slowly add the
milk, stirring continuously. Bring gently to the boil and add the
cheese and spinach, egg yolks and season to taste. Leave to cool
slightly. Whisk the egg whites into soft peaks and gently fold
into the mix. Spoon the mixture into the ramekins and place
in a roasting tin half filled with water. Bake for 15-20 minutes
until well risen and golden. Remove from oven and leave to
cool, soufflés will sink a little when they cool, this is normal. If
you don't want to make individual soufflés then you can make 1
large one using a large oven proof dish instead. Serve hot with a
green leaf salad.

Main - Italian Chicken Breast

4 chicken breasts (remove
skin)
2 oz sun blushed tomatoes
(finely chopped)
2 oz cooked rice
2 oz dolcelatte cheese

8 slices of pancetta
Knob of garlic butter

Preheat oven to 160C
Chopping board and sharp knife
Frying pan

Method

Place the chicken breasts onto a chopping board and butterfly
fillet them (cut the chicken breast to create a pocket in them).
Mix together the rice, tomatoes and dolcelatte and stuff the
chicken. Wrap the pancetta tightly around the chicken breast.
Fry in the garlic butter to seal and lightly colour. Then bake for
12-15 minutes. Serve with wilted spinach and tomato and wine
sauce.

Dessert - Lemon Tart with Raspberry Sorbet

Juice of 4 lemons
Zest of 2 lemons
650 g sugar
350 ml double cream
6 eggs
Short crust pastry

400 ml raspberry puree
4 tsp caster sugar
2 tsp red wine vinegar
200 ml milk
2 egg whites

Preheat oven to 100C
Large flan/tart baking tin
Ice cream maker

Method

Roll out the pastry into baking tin and blind bake.

To make the lemon filling: put the lemon juice, zest and sugar into the pan and bring to the boil. Add the cream and eggs mix well. Put the filling into the pastry case and bake slowly until the filling sets and the pastry is golden brown.

To make the sorbet: lightly whip the egg whites. Mix together the raspberry puree, sugar, milk and red wine vinegar. Add to the egg whites and mix in an ice cream maker until set. Store the sorbet in the freezer and eat within 1 month. Serve the tart warm with the sorbet.

Top Tip

The pastry case and sorbet can be made in advance. If you're not confident with pastry you can always cheat and buy a readymade case from the supermarket.

Thanks

Thank You...

The inspiration for this book came after I received a cook book, published by a gardening club and went to see the London production of Calendar Girls. I put the two together and the Blackthorn Villagers' Cookery Book was born.

Bruce Knox came on board at the start and as well as freely giving his time to the production of the book he also became our technical editor. I would like to thank him for this; and Michele Knox for her help and support.

Thank you also to Roberta Knox who designed the cover and also used her artistic talents on the design and layout.

Friends rallied round to help collect recipes and edit them to ensure a professional finish to the cook book. I am especially grateful to Rachel Lamont and Anne Lee for their outstanding contribution and sheer dedication to the task. Without these lassies there would be no book.

Thank you also to Georgina Grell, Karen Jobling, Susan Henderson, Teresa Bannock, Pat Tylor, Alison Webb, Ben Lee, Connie Bannock and Andy Lee for their help in making the book something we can all take pride in, throughout the village and beyond.

There are some stunning pictures within the book and these would not have been possible without the talents of Alex Grell and Bruce Knox, my thanks to both of you.

A special mention should go to the sponsors, whose generous support has paid for the publication of this book.

Also I must thank Suzanne Darvill for her support and encouragement and my friend Christine Seretny for all her help with collecting the sponsorship funds.

Thank you to Amanda Barry-Hirst for her advice and friendship and the superb PR job she has done.

Last but not least my heartfelt thanks to everyone in the village and the friends of Blackthorn for the wonderful recipes that have made this book possible.

Alexandrina Stevenson.

Index

A

B

C

D

E

F

Q

R

S

T

U

V

W

Z

Conversion Charts

Conversion Charts

Weights

(As a general rule 1 oz is roughly the equivalent to 25 g: the table below shows some common weight conversions)

Metric (g/kg)	Imperial (oz/lb)
25 g	1 oz
50 g	2 oz
75 g	3 oz
125 g	4 oz (¼ lb)
225 g	8 oz (½ lb)
350 g	12 oz (¾ lb)
450 g	6 oz (1 lb)
675 g	22 oz (1½ lb)
1 kg	2.2 lb

Cup Measures: for weight measures the important thing to remember is use the same cup for all the ingredients. American cup measures are quite complicated and depend on the ingredients.

Liquids

1 teaspoon (tsp) = 5ml
3 teaspoons (tsp) = 15 ml (1 tbsp)
1 dessertspoon (dsp) = 10ml
1 tablespoon (tbsp) = 15ml (½ fl oz)
2 tablespoons (tbsp) = 30ml (1 fl oz)

(As a general rule 1 fl oz is equivalent to 30 ml)

Metric (ml/ltr)	Imperial (fl oz/pt)
30 ml	1 fl oz
150 ml	5 fl oz (¼ pt)
300 ml	10 fl oz (½ pt)
450 ml	15 fl oz (¾ pt)
600 ml	20 fl oz (1 pt)

Cup Measures

1 cup (US) is equivalent to 8 fl oz and 237 ml
1 cup (UK) is equivalent to 10 fl oz and 300 ml

Temperature Conversions

Fahrenheit (ºF)	Celsius (ºC)	Gas Mark
275	140	1
300	150	2
325	160	3
350	180	4
375	190	5
400	200	6
425	220	7
450	230	8
475	240	9

Above are some very basic conversion tables, you can find more comprehensive ones on the internet.

Sponsors

whose generous support
funded this publication

Blackthorn Village Hall

Blackthorn Village, Thame Road

Looking for ?

Somewhere to hold a party
A place to run a keep fit class
A hall for a coffee morning

We have the perfect venue !

Whether a regular booking or one off, the management committee of Blackthorn Village Hall will always be happy to help local community groups' fund raising activities.

For more details contact

Rachel Lamont 01869 321771
Discretionary discounted rates can be applied.

Registered charity number 289348

Graphic Design and Digital Print Studio

Graphic design
Digital photography
Large format & digital printing
Marketing consultancy

Tel: 01869 868111
Email: info@advstudio.co.uk
Contact: Bruce Knox

www.advstudio.co.uk

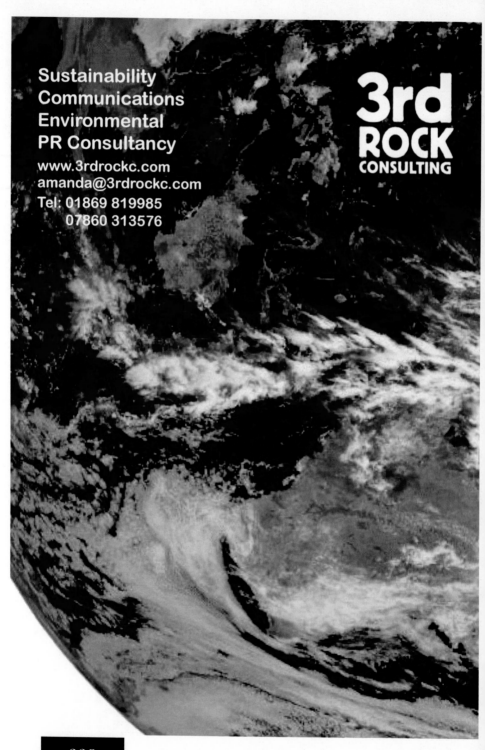

Sustainability
Communications
Environmental
PR Consultancy

www.3rdrockc.com
amanda@3rdrockc.com
Tel: 01869 819985
    07860 313576

3rd
ROCK
CONSULTING

The fastest broadband we can give you. And that's a promise.

Get up to 20Mb broadband for just £15 a month

With Virgin Media, you'll get:

- ☑ *The best speed that we can deliver down your phone line – up to 20Mb!*
- ☑ *No paying more to go faster*
- ☑ *Choose the number of downloads you want*
- ☑ *Free back-up and photo prints with V stuff*

Join today. Call our team on 0800 052 3272

TESCO Bicester

are proud to be part of the
Bicester community,
and to support the
Blackthorn Villagers
Cookery Book.

Drawn by Divine, Aged 10

Every little helps

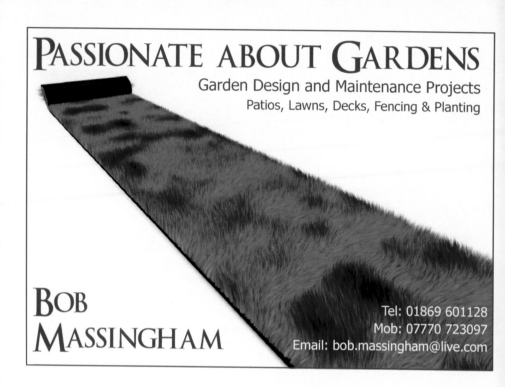

PASSIONATE ABOUT GARDENS

Garden Design and Maintenance Projects

Patios, Lawns, Decks, Fencing & Planting

BOB
MASSINGHAM

Tel: 01869 601128
Mob: 07770 723097
Email: bob.massingham@live.com

ROBERT L. DARVILL
& SON
PLASTERERS

Tel: 01869 240924   Mob: 07894 816225

robert_darvill@live.co.uk

SPACE MODULE

Secure Self-Storage
In Bicester

The ideal facility for personal customers, growing businesses and busy retailers

Space Module, Bessemer Close, Bicester, Oxfordshire OX26 6QE
01869 244487
enquiries@spacemodule.co.uk

Simon Jackson Electrical

Domestic Industrial Commercial
Electrical Installation and Repairs
Tel/Fax: 01367 718988
Mob: 07979 917001
PART P REGISTERED
Serving People in Power
www.acesparks.com

R J WAKELIN

Painting & Decorating Specialist

Interior/Exterior   Private/Commercial

01869 243264

futurewellbeing

"Want to look your stunning best, lift your whole mood and feel really good about yourself? Of course you do!"

With our unique
- Non-Surgical facial lifts,
- Patented Body Wrapping Techniques,
- XEN-Tan the celebrity favourite spray Tan,
- Superbly relaxing Body Massages.
- Jessica Manicures and Pedicures

Set yourself up to look fantastic outside, and feel wonderful inside.

Come and visit Future Wellbeing in Crown Walk, Bicester and see how we can help you achieve "THAT LOOK"
Call us on 01869 252238

futurewellbeing

"Do you want to Improve your Body?"

- Diminish Cellulite?
- Improve Poor Circulation in your Legs?
- Reduce Swollen ankles?
- Lessen Spider or Varicose Veins?

Come and have a free consultation at our clinic in Crown Walk Bicester to see if our Vacumed therapy can help you improve your Body

Call us on 01869 252238

3 Crown Walk Bicester

SOIREE DELIGHTS

www.soireedelights.co.uk

Want the Best Party in Town ?

Then why not hire a

Candy Buffet - Want a buffet with a difference?
Hire your very own Pick 'n' Mix sweet shop.

Fruit Palm Tree - An exotic alternative to any dessert
or buffet.

Chocolate Fountain - A spectacular centrepiece for
you and your guests to indulge in an exquisite chocolate
fantasy.

The Ultimate Edition to any event !

Contact abby@soireedelights.co.uk
Tel 01869 322465/07795 994180

Artizian was formed in 1997 to meet a niche requirement in the market: supplying great quality catering and support services to a range of clients.

Our success has been based on listening to our clients and having a true understanding of their' needs and culture, providing inspiring, cutting edge ideas and dynamic solutions to today's issues.

We are (relatively!) small, enabling us to make changes quickly and efficiently and be responsive to our clients' needs. As we are privately owned, we are under no pressure to grow and are able to select our clients because they share similar values to our own.

Most of all... Artizian is about individuals who have belief, passion and enthusiasm in what they do. All our people care about the business and are proud, hard working, hands on and professional. They are given the freedom to be creative and use their flair in achieving our clients' objectives - from providing fresh seasonal café food to five star hospitality services.

By developing our teams and treating our people with mutual respect we have created a service culture that is second to none.

If you would like to understand more about how Artizian may be able to help your business with its employee catering or find out what it is like working with us then please do get in touch.

The Old Barn, Spring Meadows Business Park, Wargrave, Berkshire
RG10 8PZ · Tel: 01189 404440 · Fax: 01189 404447
email: info@artizian.co.uk · www.artizian.co.uk

Artizian are delighted to have been shortlisted as a finalist in the Health, Work & Wellbeing category of the National Business Awards

eat... work... enjoy... everyday!

INVESTOR IN PEOPLE

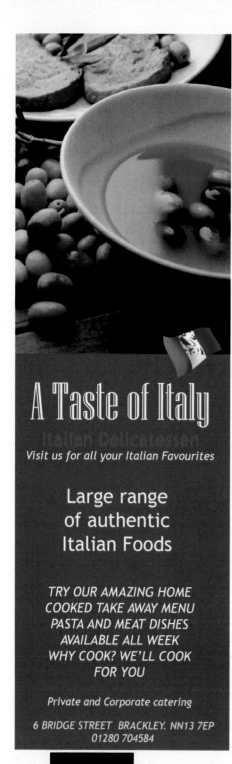

A Taste of Italy

Italian Delicatessen

Visit us for all your Italian Favourites

Large range of authentic Italian Foods

*TRY OUR AMAZING HOME
COOKED TAKE AWAY MENU
PASTA AND MEAT DISHES
AVAILABLE ALL WEEK
WHY COOK? WE'LL COOK
FOR YOU*

Private and Corporate catering

*6 BRIDGE STREET BRACKLEY. NN13 7EP
01280 704584*

WELCOME TO ANDREA AND ACHILLE

Relax in our 5 star hair salons within Oxfordshire for a unique and relaxing hair cut and colour experience.

We are Oxfordshires leading hair colour specialists and our dedicated professional team of cutters and colourists are there to fulfil your every need.

Only the best is good enough at Andrea and Achille where the needs of the individual is something we bear very much in mind

17 Crown Walk	6 Bridge street
Bicester	Brackley
01869 369058	01280 841555
1/3 West Street	8 Oxford Road
Chipping Norton	Kidlington
01608 646111	01865 374772

CAFE
Creative Activities for Elderly People

CAFE provides creative and musical sessions for elderly people in care homes in Buckinghamshire, Northamptonshire and Oxfordshire.

We offer free training and support and care homes pay all expenses. If you are interested then visit our website or give us a call. We look forward to hearing from you.

www.cafecharity.org.uk
Tel: 01280 705250
cafecharity@btinternet.com

Blackthorn Fencing Contractors

For all your domestic and commercial fencing work

Tel: 07739744242

www.blackthornfencing.co.uk

Westcote Design

Handmade
bespoke sofas
and chairs

headboards and
footstools

re-upholstery and
restoration

Tel:01608 659091
www.westcotedesign.co.uk
info@westcotedesign.co.uk

354

The Anderson Orr Partnership
Chartered Architects

We are a design led practice, dedicated to creating bespoke traditional and contemporary solutions of the highest quality. We offer a complete design service from feasibility through to completion, drawing on a wealth of experience in residential design, conservation areas and listed buildings.

Our practice is committed to the philosophy of good design, careful detailing and close personal attention to the requirements of our clients. As architects and designers we deliver exciting, creative and timeless solutions which are appropriate to the individual characteristics of each project.

Contact us for a free and informal discussion about your project

☏ 01865 873936   ✉ info@andersonorr.com   ⌂ The Studio. 70 Church Road. Wheatley. Oxford. OX33 1LZ

www.andersonorr.com

356

Mary Browning
Horse and Dog Portraits
Tel: 01295 711532

Tailor Made Catering Solutions

We are small caterers who specialize in home made dishes for a variety of events.

Why not contact us to cater for your next function?
We pride ourselves on being able to give an individual service to our customers.

June Foreman 01865 331330
Lynn Taylor 01865 331602

Email lynn.taylor25@btinternet.com

VILLAGE FABRICS

Thanks also to the following local businesses for their support and patronage:
Harlan Laboratories, Friends of Blackthorn.

SMY Electrical, Blackthorn, Tel: 01869 362 320, www.smyelectrical.co.uk

CLEAR VISION.
BESPOKE ADVICE *for our* CLIENTS.

Specialising in providing relationship based independent financial advice
Delivering a first class client service
Financial piece of mind comes to those with VISION

- Saving & Investments
- Discretionary Portfolio Management
- Inheritance Tax & Retirement Planning

- Mortgages
- Protection

Independent Financial Planning Ltd

Offices in Falmouth, Launceston, Honiton, Kent.
For an initial appointment please telephone **01326 210904** or visit **www.visionifp.co.uk**

White Horse Boiler Services
28 Joyces Road
Stanford in the Vale
Faringdon, Oxon

Professional business specialising in:-

- ✔ Gas boiler servicing
- ✔ Oil boiler servicing
- ✔ Central heating maintenance and repair
- ✔ Landlord gas safety certificates
- ✔ Boiler fault diagnosis and repair
- ✔ Boiler replacements

- ✔ No call-out fee
  - ✔ Competitive rates
    - ✔ Free quotations
      - ✔ Gas safe and Oftec registered

Call **01367 710614** to arrange an appointment.

Invite 2 or 3 of your neighbours to have their boiler serviced on the same day as you and you will each receive a £5 discount.

362

"One of the very nicest things about life is the way we must regularly stop whatever it is we are doing and devote our attention to eating."

Luciano Pavarotti, (1935 – 2007)

www.willowpond.co.uk